MODERN MYTHS ABOUT SATAN AND SPIRITUAL WARFARE

DAVID KIRKWOOD

ETHNOS PRESS
Pittsburgh, Pennsylvania

Dedication

To the wonderful people of
Grace Church of the South Hills.
Thanks for the privilege
of being your pastor.

Acknowledgments

My sincere thanks to my wife, Becky,
and my mother, LaVerne, as well as
Tony Condello and Dan Robbins,
who each unselfishly gave of themselves
to bring this book to you.

Contents

Introduction

The subject of "spiritual warfare," as you no doubt realize, has become increasingly popular in the church during the past decade. An ever-expanding number of seminars, sermons, books, and even music tapes center on this timely topic. Christians are being barraged with teachings and techniques on "pulling down strongholds over cities," "warfare prayer," "binding the strong man," and so on.

Unfortunately, much of what is being taught contradicts what Scripture teaches. Consequently, many Christians are practicing a kind of spiritual warfare that the Bible never prescribes.

As I have read some of the popular literature on the subject of spiritual warfare, I am often utterly amazed at how far some teachers have deviated from the Bible. Much of what is promoted as deeper spiritual truth is nothing but human conjecture and should be classed as false doctrine. And ironically, as false doctrines about spiritual warfare are accepted by Christians, Satan is, to some degree, accomplishing his goal to deceive believers! Some who are teaching about how to win in spiritual warfare are unwittingly helping us, through their false doctrines, to lose the very battle Satan has launched against us.

Even more alarming is the ever-increasing focus on Satan, rather than on Jesus. For some believers, practically every aspect of their Christian life centers around warfare with the devil. Their prayers begin, not with "Our Father Who art in heaven," but "Satan, I come against you now..." Praise is not thought of as something offered up to a worthy God but as something that serves as a weapon in spiritual battle. Church services are not opportunities to worship God and learn about Jesus, but times to do battle and pull down strongholds. In all of this, the devil is actually being glorified. Surely he loves all the attention.

Jesus referred to Satan as "the father of lies" (John 8:44; italics mine). Lies are the devil's primary weapon, his "fiery darts" of which the apostle Paul wrote (Eph. 6:16; KJV). Since he is the father of lies, it should not surprise us then that Satan even lies about himself. We are told by the apostle Paul that he disguises himself as an "angel of light" (2 Cor. 11:4). He wants us to believe things about himself that aren't true.

For example, Satan lies about his very existence. Many people don't believe he exists, and I think that if I were the devil, I would be quite happy about that.

Satan lies about his character. He would like us to think that he is not so evil after all—an "angel of light" if we'll accept it.

Satan lies about his operations. He wants us to believe he is much more powerful and crafty than he really is. Sadly, he has a lot of Christians fooled.

By examining the truth of Scripture, however, we can help remedy this situation. Certainly there is such a thing as *scriptural* spiritual warfare, and that is what we should be practicing. There is no reason for us to remain ignorant because the Bible tells us all we need to know about Satan and his schemes.

One of Satan's more successful schemes is to get Christians off-balance by their emphasizing one scripture at the neglect of another. Satan even attempted to use this tactic on Jesus Himself (see Matt. 4:5-7). That is why we will examine many scriptures. Much of the unscriptural teaching regarding spiritual warfare and Satan is built upon scriptures taken out of their immediate context or out of the context of what the whole Bible teaches.

It is certainly not my intention to attack any person's ministry, but simply to reveal the truth from God's Word. In the following pages, I have not mentioned anyone's name as someone who teaches error, because there is no doubt in my mind that most who are promoting unscriptural ideas about Satan and spiritual warfare are sincere and committed to Christ. Moreover, I know from personal experience the embarrassment of having to correct my own teaching. Some of the very myths which I expose in the following pages are myths I once believed and taught. I hope that no readers will think I am picking on them. We are all in this together! Please try your best to read objectively.

In the following pages I have addressed some of the most common misconceptions regarding Satan and spiritual warfare. I don't know of any one person who promotes all of these errors, so please don't assume that just because someone teaches Myth #1 that he also teaches Myth #2 and so on. What follows is a compilation of myths that have been gathered from numerous sources. In the final chapter, I discuss the essentials of biblical spiritual warfare.

My prayer is that this study will help many who need a little theological adjustment, and that it will be a blessing to those who need vital biblical information to overcome Satan's schemes in their own lives. To God be all the glory.

David Kirkwood

MYTH #1:

"In eternity past, God and Satan got into a great battle. Today, the cosmic struggle still rages between them."

This particular myth contradicts one of the most well-established, fundamental truths about God that is revealed in Scripture—the truth that He is all-powerful, or *omnipotent*, to use a theological term. From cover to cover the Bible affirms God's omnipotence.

On page one we learn that God created everything. He spoke the universe into existence. How much power did that require? Whatever the amount necessary, God had it.

Has God's power diminished since then, now that He has grown so much older? No, Jesus told us that *all things are possible* with God (Matt. 19:26). Jeremiah affirmed that there is *nothing* too difficult for Him (Jer. 32:17). No person or force can stop Him from fulfilling His plans (see 2 Chron. 20:6; Job 41:10; 42:2). Through Jeremiah God asks, "For who is like Me....And who then...can stand against Me?" (Jer. 50:44). The answer is *no one*, not even Satan.

Speaking through the prophet Isaiah, the Holy Spirit said, "Do you not know? Have you not heard? The Everlasting God, the Lord, the creator of the ends of the earth does not become weary or tired..." (Is. 40:28). Paul wrote that God is able to do "exceeding abundantly beyond all that we ask or think" (Eph 3:20).

If God is truly all-powerful as the above-mentioned scriptures affirm, then to say that God and Satan were or are in a battle is to imply that He is *not* all-powerful. If God lost even a single round, or was slightly overcome by Satan even to a small degree, or had to struggle against him for even a short time, then He is not all-powerful, as He declares Himself to be.

Christ's Commentary on Satan's Power

Jesus once said something concerning Satan's fall from heaven that will help us understand how much power Satan has in comparison to our omnipotent God:

> And the seventy returned with joy, saying, "Lord, even the demons are subject to us in Your name." And He said to them, "I was watching Satan fall from heaven like lightning" (Luke 10:17-18).

When Jesus sent out seventy of His disciples to preach and heal, they returned exuberantly to report that even the demons were subject to them in His name. They should not have been so surprised, however. Jesus informed them that in His preincarnate state, He had witnessed a very revealing demonstration of the Father's supreme power over Satan: When the all-powerful God decreed Satan's expulsion from heaven, *Satan could not resist.* Jesus chose the metaphor, *like lightning,* to emphasize the speed with which Satan fell. He fell, not *like molasses,* but *like lightning.* He didn't fall like a leaf from a tree or a rock from a cliff. Oh no. Satan was in heaven one second, and in the next—BOOM!—he was out of there!

If God can so quickly and easily expel Satan himself, it should have been no surprise that His commissioned servants could also quickly and easily expel demons.

Previously, those disciples possessed great respect for the horrible power that demons exercised over their victims, but now they had witnessed *a far greater power*, causing their joyful amazement. How some of us need this same revelation. Too many Christians have a great respect for the power of the devil and have not yet grasped that God's power is far, far, *far* greater. God is the Creator, and Satan is only a creation.

Satan is no match for God. There is no comparison between God's power and Satan's power. Satan cannot even struggle against God's great power, as Jesus so aptly put it.

The War That Never Was

As strange as it may seem to some of our ears, we need to understand that *God and Satan are not, have never been, and never will be in a battle.* Yes, they do have differing agendas, and perhaps it could be cautiously said that they are in opposition. But when two parties are in opposition to one another, and one is immensely more powerful than the other, their conflicts are not considered battles. Could an earthworm fight with an elephant? An earthworm might make a very feeble attempt to oppose an elephant, but their contention could hardly be described as a fight.

Satan, like that earthworm, made a feeble attempt to oppose One who was immensely more powerful. His opposition was quickly dealt with, and he was expelled from heaven "like lightning." There was no battle—there was only an expulsion.

If God is all-powerful, then Satan doesn't have a ghost of a chance at slightly hindering God from doing what He wants to do. And if God does permit Satan to do something, ultimately it is only to accomplish His own divine will. This truth will become abundantly clear as we continue to examine the Scriptures in later chapters.

Obviously, God permitted Satan to make a choice regarding obedience or disobedience, which is what theologians call *free will*. But the only reason Satan possessed the authority to make a choice was because God gave him that authority.

The Future Binding of Satan

God's supreme authority over Satan was not only demonstrated in eternity past, but will also be demonstrated in the future. We read in Revelation that *one angel* will bind Satan and incarcerate him for one thousand years:

> And I saw an angel coming down from heaven, having the key of the abyss and a great chain in his hand. And he laid hold of the dragon, the serpent of old, who is the devil and Satan, and bound him for a thousand years, and threw him into the abyss, and shut it and sealed it over him, so that he should not deceive the nations any longer, until the thousand years were completed; after these things he must be released for a short time (Rev. 20:1-3).

This future incident could not be considered a battle between God and Satan any more than Satan's original expulsion from heaven could be considered a battle between God and Satan. This unnamed angel will simply lay hold of Satan and put him out of operation for a thousand years. There is no mention of any skirmish.

Notice also that Satan will not have the power to break out of his prison and will only be released when it suits God's purposes (see Rev. 20:7-9).

God could easily bind Satan right now if He desired. To say that He could not is to say that He is not more powerful than Satan.

Then why doesn't God put a stop to Satan right now? Simply because it does not suit His purposes at this time. There are reasons why God permits Satan to function upon the earth, reasons which we will explore in later chapters.[1]

What About the Future "War in Heaven"?

If it is true that God and Satan are not, have never been, and never will be in a battle, then why do we read in the book of Revelation of a future war in heaven that involves

---

[1] Some claim that God cannot stop Satan right now because Satan usurped Adam's authority and now possesses Adam's former right to rule the earth, a right that God cannot revoke. This is a myth about Satan we will examine in the third chapter.

Satan? That's a good question, and one that can be answered without any trouble. Let's first read about that future heavenly war in Revelation 12:7-9:

> And there was war in heaven, Michael and his angels waging war with the dragon. And the dragon and his angels waged war, and they were not strong enough, and there was no longer a place found for them in heaven. And the great dragon was thrown down, the serpent of old who is called the devil and Satan, who deceives the whole world; he was thrown down to the earth, and his angels were thrown down with him (Rev. 12:7-9).

If you will read the verses which immediately precede and follow those quoted above, you will see that this incident of which John wrote is not a description of Satan's *original* expulsion from heaven, when he "fell like lightning." Rather, it is a description of a *future* expulsion.[2] Other scriptures indicate that Satan, even since his original expulsion, may still have some limited access to God's heaven (see Job 1:6; 2:1; Zech. 3:1-2, Luke 22:31; Rev. 12:10).

Notice that this war will be between *Michael and his angels and Satan and his angels*. God Himself is not mentioned as being involved in the battle. If He were, the conflict could hardly be described as a war, because God, being all-powerful, could easily squelch any opposition in a flash of time as He has already proven.

Angels, including Michael, are not all-powerful, and thus their conflict with Satan and his angels can be described as a war because there will be some actual conflict for a portion of time. Still, they, being more powerful, will overcome Satan and his hordes.

Why would God not become personally involved in this particular battle, leaving it to His angels? I have no idea.

---

[2] For example, 12:10 reads, "And I heard a loud voice in heaven, saying, '*Now* the salvation, and the power, and the kingdom of our God and the authority of His Christ have come, *for the accuser of our brethren has been thrown down, who accuses them before our God day and night*'" (italics mine). When Satan was originally expelled from heaven, there were no brethren to accuse.

Certainly God, being all-knowing, knew that His angels could win the war, and so perhaps He figured there was no need for Him to be involved personally. And I suppose that if God did everything Himself, the angels would have nothing to do!

I have no doubt that God could have easily and quickly annihilated the wicked Canaanites in the days of Joshua, but He chose to give the Israelites the task. What God could have done effortlessly in seconds He required them to do, expending great efforts over a period of months. Perhaps this was more pleasing to God as it required faith on the part of the Israelites. Perhaps that is the reason He will not be personally involved in that future war in heaven. The Bible, however, does not tell us why.

Just because there is going to be a war someday in heaven between Michael and his angels and Satan and his angels is no reason for us to think that God is not all-powerful—any more than Israel's battles in Canaan are reason for us to think that God is not all-powerful. Remember, God's angels are not all-powerful—God is.

Was Not Satan Defeated by Jesus on the Cross?

In regard to this first myth of God and Satan's supposed battles, I would like to conclude this chapter by addressing the commonly used statement: *Jesus defeated Satan on the cross.*

I had often stated that Jesus defeated Satan on the cross until I realized that what I was saying was not entirely accurate according to the Bible. Scripture never actually states that Jesus *defeated* Satan on the cross.

You may think I'm splitting theological hairs, but there is good reason to be so particular. When we say that Jesus *defeated* Satan, we make it sound as if they were in a battle, which implies that God is not all-powerful and that Satan was not already under the complete authority of God. That is why I no longer say that Jesus *defeated* Satan on the Cross. There are more biblical ways of describing what happened to Satan when Jesus gave His life on Calvary.

Hebrews 2:14-15 tells us: "Since then the children [that's us, the children of God] share in flesh and blood [that is, we have physical bodies], He Himself [Jesus] likewise also partook of the same [a physical body], that through death *He might render powerless him who had the power of death*, that is, the devil; and might deliver those who through fear of death were subject to slavery all their lives" (italics mine).

We read that Jesus, through His death, rendered Satan *powerless*. To what extent did He render Satan powerless? Obviously, Satan is not *completely* powerless, or else the apostle John would never have written that "the whole world lies in the *power* of the evil one" (1 John 5:19; italics mine). Neither would James and Peter have told us to resist the devil, because, if Satan had no power, there would be nothing for us to resist (see James 4:7; 1 Pet. 5:8-9). Nor would Paul have written, "And the God of peace will soon crush Satan under your feet" (Rom. 16:20).

If you were passing by and overheard me say to someone, "I'm powerless," you wouldn't necessarily think I meant that I was incapable of doing *anything*. You would assume that I meant I was perhaps powerless to change a certain situation, or that I had lost some jurisdiction over something I had previously controlled. If you had heard the context of my comment, you would probably know exactly what I meant. This is why it is so important to read verses of the Bible within their context, otherwise, we can wrongly interpret what God is trying to communicate to us.

We have already determined from other scriptures that Satan was not rendered totally powerless or inoperable by Jesus' death. Thus we need to know in what area or to what extent Satan was rendered powerless. Hebrews 2:14-15 tells us. It says that through His death, Jesus rendered "powerless him who had the *power of death*, that is, the devil; and might deliver those who through fear of death were subject to slavery all their lives" (italics mine). Satan was rendered powerless in regard to "*the power of death*."

What, exactly, does that mean?

This question is answered by looking at what other parts of the New Testament have to say about death.

Three Kinds of Death

Scripture makes reference to three kinds of death: *spiritual death, physical death*, and *the second death*.

The *second death* (or *eternal death*) is referred to in Revelation 2:22; 20:6,14; 21:8, and is described as the time when unbelievers will be thrown into the lake of fire.

Physical death occurs when a person's spirit departs from his body, and his body then ceases to function.

Scripture teaches that we are tripartite in nature: spirit, soul, and body (see 1 Thes. 5:23). Our body is our physical person, the flesh and bones and blood. Our soul is our emotions, intellect and will. Our spirit is referred to in Scripture as "the inward man" (2 Cor. 4:16), or "the hidden man of the heart" (1 Pet. 3:4). In both cases, the spirit is called a "man." The spirit is not a cloud or an attitude; it is a person. The spirit has been described by some as the "real you." Your spirit-man is eternal.

With this in mind we can better understand the third kind of death of which the Bible speaks—spiritual death.

Being *spiritually dead* describes the condition of a human spirit which has not been born again by the Holy Spirit. A spiritually dead person has a spirit which is alienated from God, a spirit which possesses a sinful nature, a spirit which is, to some degree, joined to Satan. Ephesians 2:1-3 paints for us a picture of the spiritually dead man:

> And you were dead in your trespasses and sins, in which you formerly walked according to the course of this world, according to the prince of the power of the air, of the spirit that is now working in the sons of disobedience. Among them we too all formerly lived in the lusts of our flesh, indulging the desires of the flesh and of the mind, and were by nature children of wrath, even as the rest.

Paul said the Ephesian Christians were *dead* in their trespasses and sins. Obviously he was not referring to physical death because he was writing to physically alive people. Therefore, he must have been saying that they were dead, spiritually speaking.

What killed them, spiritually? It was their "trespasses and sins." Remember God told Adam that in the day he disobeyed, he would die (Gen. 2:17). God was not speaking of physical death, but spiritual death, because Adam did not die physically on the day he ate the forbidden fruit. Rather, he died spiritually that day, and did not die physically until hundreds of years later.

Paul continued by saying that the Ephesians, as spiritually dead people, had walked in (or practiced) those trespasses and sins, following the "course of the world" (that is, doing what everyone else was doing) and following "the prince of the power of the air."

Who is "the prince of the power of the air"? He is Satan, who rules his dark domain as commander-in-chief over other evil spirits who inhabit the atmosphere. Those evil spirits are listed by rank in a later chapter of Ephesians (see Eph. 6:12).

Paul said that dark prince is a "spirit that is now working in the sons of disobedience." The expression, "sons of disobedience," is just another description for all unbelievers which emphasizes that their very nature is sinful. Paul later said that they "were *by nature* children of wrath" (Eph. 2:3; italics mine). Additionally, he said that Satan was working *in* them.

The Devil for a Dad

Whether unsaved people realize it or not, they are following Satan and are his subjects in the kingdom of darkness. They have his evil, selfish nature residing in their spiritually dead spirits. Satan is actually their spiritual lord and father. That is why Jesus once said to some unsaved religious leaders: "You are of your father the devil, and you want to do the desires of your father" (John 8:44).

This is the bleak picture of the person who has not been born again! He is walking through life spiritually dead, full of Satan's nature, heading for an inevitable physical death which he greatly fears; and, whether he realizes it or not, he will one day experience the worst death of all, eternal death, as he is cast into the lake of fire to suffer there forever.

It is extremely important that we understand that spiritual, physical, and eternal death are all manifestations of God's wrath upon sinful humanity, and that Satan has a part in all of it. Satan has been permitted by God to rule over the kingdom of darkness and over all those who "love the darkness" (John 3:19). In effect, God said to Satan, "You may hold in captivity through your power those who are not submitted to Me." Satan became a subordinate instrument of God's wrath upon human rebels. Because all have sinned, all are under Satan's power, filled with his nature in their spirits and held captive to do his will (see 2 Tim. 2:26).

The Ransom for Our Captivity

We can thank God, however, that He had mercy upon humanity, and because of His mercy, no one has to remain in that pitiful condition! Because Jesus' substitutionary death satisfied the claims of divine justice, all those who believe in Christ can escape from spiritual death and Satan's captivity because they are no longer under God's wrath. When we put our faith in Jesus, the Holy Spirit comes into our spirits and eradicates Satan's nature from it, causing our spirits to be born again (see John 3:1-16) and allowing us to become partakers of God's divine nature! (see 2 Pet. 1:4).

Now back to our original question. When the writer of Hebrews stated that Jesus, through His death, rendered "powerless him who had the power of death, that is, the devil," he meant that the power of *spiritual* death, which Satan holds over every unsaved person, has been broken over all those who are "in Christ." We are made spiritually alive because of Christ; He has paid the penalty for our sins.

Moreover, because we are no longer spiritually dead and under Satan's dominion, we no longer have to fear *physical* death, since we know what awaits us—a glorious inheritance in heaven. Some of us may even *escape* physical death—if we are alive when Jesus returns (see 1 Cor. 15:51; 1 Thes. 4:13-18).

Finally, because of Jesus, we have been delivered from suffering the *second death*, being cast into the lake of fire.

Did Jesus *defeat* the devil on the cross? No, He did not, because there was no battle between Jesus and Satan. Jesus did, however, render Satan powerless in regard to Satan's power over spiritual death, by which he holds unsaved people captive in sin. Satan still holds the power of spiritual death over unsaved people, but as far as those who are in Christ are concerned, Satan is powerless over them. This is why in Revelation 12:11, we read, "And they [the believers] overcame him [Satan] because of the blood of the Lamb." *It was because Jesus shed His blood on the cross that we have overcome Satan.*

The Disarming of the Powers

This also helps us understand Paul's statement about the "disarming of rulers and authorities" found in Colossians 2:13-15:

> And when you were [spiritually] dead in your transgressions...He made you alive together with Him, having forgiven us all our transgressions, having canceled out the certificate of debt consisting of decrees against us and which was hostile to us; and He has taken it out of the way, having nailed it to the cross. When He had disarmed the rulers and authorities, He made a public display of them, having triumphed over them through Him.

Paul uses obvious metaphorical language in this passage. In the first part, he compares our guilt to a "certificate of debt." What we could not pay was paid for us by Christ, who took our sin-debt to the cross. There our account was paid in full.

In the second part, just as ancient kings stripped their defeated foes of their weapons and triumphantly paraded them through their city streets, so Christ's death was a triumph over "rulers and authorities," the lower ranks of demons who rule over rebellious humans, holding them captive.

Could we not say, based upon this passage, that Christ *defeated* Satan? Perhaps, but with some qualification. We must keep in mind that, in this passage, Paul was writing metaphorically. And every metaphor, whether written or spoken, has a point where the similarities turn to dissimilarities.

For example, if I say to my wife, "Your eyes are like pools," I mean that her eyes are deep, dark, blue, and inviting. But I mean nothing more, because those are the only similarities between my wife's eyes and pools of water. I did not mean that fish swim in her eyes, or that they freeze over in the winter, or that ducks might want to land on them. Every metaphor is like that. It reaches a point where, if pushed beyond the intended similarities, would darken understanding rather then enlighten it, as metaphors are supposed to do. (This very thing is often done by people trying to find some significance in every minor detail of Jesus' parables, when Jesus was usually only trying to make one major point.)

In interpreting Paul's metaphors in Colossians 2:13-15, we must be equally cautious. Obviously, there wasn't an actual "certificate of debt" that had all our sins written on it that was nailed to the cross. That is, however, symbolic of what Jesus accomplished.

By the same token, the demons who ruled over unsaved humanity were not literally disarmed of their swords and shields and paraded publicly through the streets by Jesus. The language Paul uses is symbolic of what Jesus accomplished for us. We were held captive by those evil spirits, but, by dying for our sins, Jesus released us from our captivity. Jesus didn't literally fight against those evil spirits and they were not at war with Him. They, by God's righteous permission, held *us* in their power all of our lives. Their "armaments," as it were, were pointed, not at Christ, but at us. Jesus, however, "disarmed" them. They can't keep us captive any longer.

Let us not think that there was some age-long fight between Jesus and Satan's evil spirits, and finally, Jesus won the battle on the cross. If we are going to say that Jesus defeated the devil, let us be certain we understand that He defeated the devil *for us*, and not for Himself. He didn't need to overcome the devil for Himself.

In my front yard I once chased away a small dog who was terrifying my baby daughter. I might say I *defeated* that little dog, but I hope you understand that dog was never any threat to me, only to my daughter. It was the same with Jesus and Satan. Jesus chased away a dog from us that never bothered Him at all.

How did He chase away that Satan-dog? He did it by bearing the punishment for our sins, thus releasing us from our guilt before God, thus delivering us from God's wrath, and thus the evil spirits whom God righteously permits to enslave human rebels no longer had any right to enslave us. Praise God for that!

Myth #1: "In eternity past, God and Satan got into a great battle. Today, the cosmic struggle still rages between them."

No, we can thank God that in eternity past Satan was *expelled* from heaven *without a fight*. God will someday, through one powerful angel, bind Satan and render him inoperable for a thousand years. In the meantime, Satan's power in holding people captive through spiritual death has been broken over all those who are in Christ. Satan is no longer our spiritual father and lord. God Himself is not, never has been, and never will be in a battle with Satan. *God is all-powerful.* Hallelujah!

This leads us to an appropriate place to examine a second related myth.

MYTH #2:

"There are constant battles in the spiritual realm between God's angels and Satan's angels. The outcome of those battles is determined by our 'spiritual warfare.'"

In the last chapter, we learned from the book of Revelation that one day there will be a war in heaven between Michael and his angels and Satan and his angels. Other than that, there is only *one* other angelic battle which Scripture mentions, found in the tenth chapter of Daniel.[1]

Daniel tells us that he had been mourning for three weeks during the third year of the reign of Cyrus, king of

---

[1] Two possible objections answered: (1) Jude mentions a dispute between Michael and Satan about the body of Moses, but there is no mention of an actual battle. In fact, Jude tells us that Michael would "not dare pronounce against him [Satan] a railing judgment, but said, 'The Lord rebuke you'" (Jude 1:9). (2) When Elisha and his servant were surrounded by a Syrian army in the city of Dothan, Elisha prayed for God to open his servant's eyes (2 Kings 6:15-17). Consequently, his servant saw "horses and chariots of fire" which we assume were mounted and occupied by an army of angels in the spiritual realm. This is not, however, a definite indication that these angels had been or were about to be involved in a battle with demonic angels. Angels are used at times by God to execute His wrath against wicked human beings, an example being the slaughter of 185,000 Assyrian soldiers by one angel, recorded in 2 Kings 19:35.

Persia, when an angel appeared to him by the Tigris River. The purpose of the angel's visit was to impart to him understanding concerning Israel's future. During their conversation, the unnamed angel said to Daniel:

> "Do not be afraid, Daniel, for from the first day that you set your heart on understanding this and on humbling yourself before your God, your words were heard, and I have come in response to your words. But the *prince of the kingdom of Persia* was withstanding me for twenty-one days; *then behold, Michael, one of the chief princes, came to help me,* for I had been left there with the kings of Persia" (Dan. 10:12-13; italics mine).

Daniel learned that his prayer had been been heard three weeks prior to his encounter with this angel, but that it had taken the angel three weeks to get to him. The reason for the angel's delay was because "the prince of the kingdom of Persia" had withstood him. He was able to break through, however, when Michael, "one of the chief princes," came to help him.

When the angel was about to depart from Daniel, he said to him,

> "Do you understand why I came to you? But I shall now return to fight against the prince of Persia; so I am going forth, and behold, the prince of Greece is about to come. However, I will tell you what is inscribed in the writing of truth. Yet there is no one who stands firmly with me against these forces except Michael your prince" (Dan. 10:20-21).

Several interesting facts can be learned from this passage of Scripture. Again we see that God's angels are not all-powerful, and that they can actually be involved in fighting wicked angels. (It would be interesting to know just how spirit-beings fight, wouldn't it? Frank Peretti's fictional works certainly have supplied us with vivid images to fill our imaginations.)

Second, we learn that some angels (such as Michael) are more powerful than others (such as the one who spoke with Daniel).

Questions For Which We Have No Answers

We may ask, "Why didn't God send *Michael* with the message for Daniel in the first place so that there would not have been a three-week delay?" We don't know the answer to that question. *Perhaps* there was something God wanted that particular angel to learn. Angels are not all-knowing, and thus would have the capacity to gain more knowledge if God so willed it. Scripture tells us they are curious (see 1 Pet. 1:12).

Or, perhaps God wanted Daniel to learn perseverance in prayer.

The fact is, however, that the Bible doesn't tell us why God sent an angel whom He *undoubtedly knew* would not be able to break past the "prince of Persia" without the help of Michael. In fact, we have no idea why God would use *any* angel to deliver a message to someone! Why didn't He go personally, or speak to Daniel audibly, or bring Daniel temporarily to heaven to tell him? We just don't know the answers.

But does this passage prove that there are constant battles in the spiritual realm between God's angels and Satan's angels? No, it only proves that, several thousand years ago, there was *one three-week struggle* between one of God's weaker angels and one of Satan's angels named "the prince of Persia," a battle, which, if God had so willed, would never have occurred. *The only other angelic battle mentioned in all of the Bible is the one future war in heaven, recorded in the book of Revelation.* That's it. There *may* have been other angelic battles that have occurred, but it would be an assumption on our part to so conclude.

Quite obviously, the subject of angelic battles in the spiritual realm is not nearly as important as some make it out to be, as proven by the fact that there is so little reference to the subject in the Bible. How this could become the primary focus of a church or someone's ministry is difficult to understand.

A Myth Based Upon a Myth

Does this story of Daniel and the prince of Persia prove that our spiritual warfare can determine the outcome of angelic battles? Again, this idea *assumes* (based upon a few scriptures) that there *are* regular angelic battles! But let's take a leap in the dark and say that, yes, there are regular angelic battles. Does this story about Daniel prove that our spiritual warfare can determine the outcome of angelic battles that perhaps do occur?

The question is often asked by those who promote this particular myth, "What if Daniel had given up after one day?" The answer to that question, of course, no one actually knows, because the fact is that Daniel didn't stop seeking God in prayer until the unnamed angel arrived. The implication in asking it, however, is to convince us that Daniel, through continued spiritual warfare, was the key to the unnamed angel's breakthrough in the heavenlies. If Daniel had quit doing spiritual battle, supposedly the angel would never have made it past the prince of Persia. They want us to believe that we, like Daniel, must continue in spiritual battle, or else some evil angel may triumph over one of God's angels.

First, may I point out that Daniel was not "doing spiritual warfare"—he was *praying to God*. There is no mention of him saying anything to any demonic angels, or binding them, or "warring" against them. Daniel, in fact, *had no knowledge that there was any on-going angelic battle until three weeks had passed and the unnamed angel appeared to him*. He spent those three weeks fasting and seeking God.

So let us rephrase the question: If Daniel had quit praying and seeking God after one or two days, would that unnamed angel have failed to get God's message through to him? We don't know. May I point out, however, that the unnamed angel never said to Daniel, "It's a good thing you kept praying, or else I would never had made it." No, the angel gave credit to *Michael* for his breakthrough. Obviously it was *God* who sent the unnamed angel *and* Michael, and He sent them in response to Daniel's prayer for understanding of what was to take place in Israel's future.

It would be an assumption to think that if Daniel had stopped fasting or seeking God, God would have said, "O.K. you two angels, Daniel has stopped fasting and praying, so even though I sent one of you to take a message to him on the first day he started praying, forget about getting that message to Daniel. It looks like there never will be an eleventh or twelfth chapter in Daniel's book."

Daniel obviously did persevere in *prayer* (not "spiritual warfare"), and God responded by sending angels. We, too, should persevere in prayer to God, and if God so wills, our answer could come by the agency of an angel. Angels exist, at least in part, to assist God and us! (see Heb. 1:13-14). But don't forget that there are plenty of examples of angels delivering important messages to biblical people where no mention is made of anyone praying a single prayer, much less praying for three weeks.[2] We need to stay balanced on this. Furthermore, there are scores of instances of angels who gave messages to biblical people that include no mention of those angels having to fight demonic angels on the way from heaven. Those angels *may* have had to fight evil angels in order to deliver their messages, but if they did, we don't know about it, because the Bible doesn't tell us.

A scripture quite worthy of our remembrance is also one that is very appropriate in ending this chapter: "The secret things belong to the Lord our God, but the things revealed belong to us and to our sons forever..." (Deut. 29:29). Let's walk in the light of what God has revealed to us in His Word and let Him keep His secrets. Battles between God's angels and Satan's angels make for great fiction, but you shouldn't base your prayer-life upon fiction.

---

[2] See, for example, Matt. 1:20; 2:13,19; 4:11; Luke 1:11-20, 26-38.

Myth #2: "There are constant battles in the spiritual realm between God's angels and Satan's angels. The outcome of those battles is determined by our 'spiritual warfare.'"

The truth is that we know of only *one* angelic battle in the past and *one* that will occur in the future. *If* there are any others, there is no biblical evidence that we can do "spiritual warfare" and help God's angels win their battles. When our prayers are in accordance with God's will, they can, of course, make a big difference as to what happens on this earth. And if in answering our prayers God decides to use angels, that is His business. From the very limited amount of Scripture dedicated to the subject, it is obvious that God does not want our focus to be on angelic warfare.

MYTH #3:

"When Adam Fell, Satan Got Adam's Lease to Control the World."

What exactly did happen to Satan at the fall of humanity? Some think that Satan gained a big promotion when Adam fell. They say Adam was originally "the god of this world," but at his fall Satan gained that position, thus giving him the right to do whatever he wanted on the earth. Even God was powerless to stop him from then on, because Adam had the "legal right" to give his position to Satan, and God had to honor His agreement with Adam which now belonged to Satan. Satan supposedly now possesses "Adam's lease," and God can't stop Satan until "Adam's lease runs out."

Is this theory true? Did Satan gain "Adam's lease" at the fall of humanity? Absolutely not. Satan gained nothing at the fall of humanity except a curse from God's own mouth and a divine promise of his total demise. He was already a supreme loser as one who previously possessed a place in heaven but was expelled. Then, at Adam's fall, God cursed him, promising him that one day his head would be crushed by the "seed of the woman," that is Christ. Satan was an outcast-loser who became a cursed and doomed outcast-loser!

Satan's-Gain Theory Disproved

Let's examine, in the light of Scripture, the commonly-believed myth that Satan won an upper hand in controlling the world at the fall of man and even gained an authority that was outside God's jurisdiction.

First, the Bible *never* says that Adam was the original "god of this world." Second, the Bible *never* says that Adam had a legal right to give anyone else his supposed authority over the world. You won't find such an idea taught by Paul, Peter, James, John, Jude, or Jesus. Third, the Bible *never* says that Adam had a lease that would one day expire. *All* of these ideas are unscriptural.

What authority did Adam originally possess? We read in Genesis that God told Adam and Eve to "be fruitful and multiply, and fill the earth, and *subdue* it; and *rule over the fish of the sea and over the birds of the sky, and over every living thing that moves on the earth*" (Gen. 1:28; italics mine).

God said nothing to Adam about being a "god" over the earth, or that he could control *everything*, such as the weather, and all the future people who would be born, and so on. He simply gave both Adam and Eve, as the first humans, dominion over the fish, birds and animals and commanded them to fill the earth and subdue it.

When God pronounced judgment upon the man, He said nothing about Adam losing his supposed position as "god of this world." Moreover, He said nothing to Adam or Eve about losing their dominion over fish, birds and cattle! In fact, I think it is obvious that humanity is still ruling over the fish and birds and "every creeping thing." The human race is still filling the earth and subduing it. Adam lost none of his original, God-given authority at the fall.

Isn't Satan "God of This World"?

But didn't Paul refer to Satan as the "god of this world,"

and Jesus refer to him as "ruler of this world"? Yes they did, but neither made *any* intimation that Adam was formerly "the god of this world" or that Satan gained the title from Adam when he fell.

Additionally, Satan's title as "god of this world" does not prove that Satan can do anything he wants on the earth and that God is powerless to stop him. Jesus said, "*All* authority has been given to Me in heaven *and on earth*" (Matt. 28:18; italics mine). Was He telling the truth? If He was, then that should be the end of any theory that God would like to stop Satan, but can't because Satan has "Adam's lease." If Jesus has *all* authority on the earth, then Satan can operate only with *His* permission.

Who gave Jesus all authority in heaven and on earth? It must have been God the Father, who possessed it Himself in order to give it to Jesus. That is why Jesus spoke of His Father as "Lord of heaven *and earth*" (Matt 11:25; Luke 10:21; italics mine). These two scriptures alone should be enough to convince us of the fallacy of thinking that Satan has authority outside of God's jurisdiction.

God has had all authority over the earth since He created it. He gave a little authority to humans at the beginning, and humanity has never lost what God originally gave. Man is still filling the earth and subduing it; he is still ruling over the animal kingdom.

When the Bible speaks of Satan being the god or ruler of this world, it simply means that the people of the world (who are not born again) are following Satan. He is the one they are serving, whether they realize it or not. He is their god.

The Bible informs us that there are only two families of people from a spiritual perspective, the children of God and the children of the devil (1 Jn. 3:10). Satan is the god and spiritual father of all unsaved people (Jn. 8:44, Eph. 2:2). He is only ruling the kingdom of darkness, and that with God's permission. Just because Satan is called "the god of this world" does not mean that he can do anything he wants to do on the earth, or that he is not under God's authority.

Satan's Real-Estate Offer?

Much of the Satan-Gained theory is built upon the story of Satan's temptation of Jesus in the wilderness, recorded by Matthew and Luke. Let's examine Luke's account to see what we can learn:

> And he [Satan] led Him [Jesus] up and showed Him all the kingdoms of the world in a moment of time. And the devil said to Him, "I will give You all this domain and its glory; for it has been handed over to me, and I give it to whomever I wish. Therefore if You worship before me, it shall all be Yours." And Jesus answered and said to him, "It is written, 'You shall worship the Lord your God and serve Him only'" (Luke 4:5-8).

Does this incident prove that Satan has control over *everything* in the world, or that Adam handed it over to him, or that God is powerless to stop the devil? No, it does not, for a number of good reasons.

First of all, we should be careful about basing our theology upon a statement made by someone whom Jesus called "the father of lies" (John 8:44). I recognize that Satan sometimes does tell the truth, but in this case, our warning flag should be waving furiously, because what Satan said apparently contradicts something that God has said.

In the fourth chapter of the book of Daniel, we read the story of King Nebuchadnezzar's humiliation. Nebuchadnezzar, full of pride over his position and accomplishments, was told by the prophet Daniel that he would be given the mind of an animal until he recognized that *"the Most High is ruler over the realm of mankind, and bestows it on whomever He wishes"* (Dan. 4:25; italics mine). Four times this same declaration is made in connection with this story, underscoring its importance (Dan. 4:17, 25, 32; 5:21). God wanted Nebuchadnezzar to know that he was a ruler *only* because God had exalted him, and thus he had no valid reason to be proud.

Notice that Daniel said that *"the Most High is ruler over*

the realm of mankind." That indicates God has some control on the earth, doesn't it?

Notice also that Daniel's claim seems to be a direct contradiction of what Satan said to Jesus. Daniel said God "bestows it on whomever He wishes," and Satan said, "I give it to whomever I wish" (Luke 4:6).

So who are you going to believe? Personally, I'm going to believe Daniel! Satan could be the spiritual equivalent of the guy who tried to sell the Brooklyn Bridge!

There is, however, a possibility that Satan was telling the truth—if we look at what he said from a different angle.

Satan is "the god of this world," which, as I have already stated, means that he is ruling over the kingdom of darkness, which includes people in every nation who are in rebellion against God. The Bible states that "the whole world lies in the power of the evil one" (1 John 5:19). When Satan claimed he could give authority over the kingdoms of the earth to whomever he wished, he could very well have been speaking *only of his own domain, the kingdom of darkness*, which is made up of sub-kingdoms that roughly correspond to geopolitical kingdoms. We are informed by Scripture that Satan has several ranks of evil spirits through which he rules his kingdom (see Eph. 6:12), and could assume that he is the one who promotes or demotes those spirits within his ranks, as he is the top dog. In that case, Satan was legitimately offering Jesus the position of number-two evil spirit—after himself—to help him rule his dark kingdom. All Jesus had to do was fall before Satan and worship him. Thankfully, Jesus passed that opportunity for "advancement"![1]

Who Gave Satan His Authority?

But what about Satan's claim that the authority of those kingdoms had been "handed over" to him?

Again, there is the very real possibility that Satan was lying. But let's give him the benefit of the doubt and assume he was telling the truth.

---

[1] And may I add, "O Hallelujah!"

Notice Satan did not say that *Adam* had handed it over to him. As we have already seen, Adam couldn't have handed it over to Satan because Adam never had it to give. Adam ruled fish, birds, and cattle, not kingdoms. (There were, in fact, no kingdoms of people to rule when Adam fell.) Additionally, if, as I have described, Satan was offering Jesus rule over the kingdom of darkness, which consisted of all evil spirits and unsaved people, then there is *absolutely* no way that Adam could have handed that jurisdiction over to Satan. Satan was ruling over fallen angels before Adam was created.

Satan *may* have meant that all the people of the world had handed him authority over them, as they were not submitted to God and thus were, knowingly or unknowingly, submitted to him.

An even better possibility, which may seem strange to you at this point, but which will make much more sense when we later learn why God permits Satan to do anything on the earth, is that *God* handed it over to him. It is very possible, in the light of Scripture, that God said to Satan, "You and your evil spirits have My permission to rule over everyone who is not submitted to Me." Again, that may seem hard for you to swallow now, but you will see later that is probably the best explanation of Satan's claim that his authority had been handed over to him. If God truly is "ruler over the realm of mankind" (Dan. 4:25), then any authority Satan has over mankind *must* have been granted by God.

Satan is only ruling the kingdom of darkness, which could also be called the "kingdom of rebellion." He was ruling over that kingdom since the day he was expelled from heaven, which was prior to Adam's fall. Up until Adam's fall, the kingdom of darkness consisted only of angelic rebels. But when Adam sinned, he joined the kingdom of rebellion, and Satan's kingdom ever since then has included not just rebellious angels, but rebellious humans.

Satan had rule over his dark domain before Adam was

even created, and so let us not think that when Adam fell, Satan gained something that Adam previously possessed. No, when Adam sinned, he joined a kingdom of rebellion that had existed for some time, a kingdom ruled by Satan.

Was God Surprised by the Fall?

Another flaw in the "Satan's-Gain theory" is that it makes God look rather stupid, as if He was caught off-guard by the events of the fall and as a result found Himself in a sad predicament. Did God not know that Satan would tempt Adam and Eve and that the fall of man would result? If God is all-knowing, and He is, then He must have known what was going to happen. That is why the Bible informs us that He made plans to redeem humanity even before He created humanity (see Matt. 25:34; Acts 2:2-23; 4:27-28; 1 Cor. 2:7-8; Eph. 3:8-11; 2 Tim. 1:8-10; Rev. 13:8).

God created the devil knowing he would fall, and He created Adam and Eve knowing they would fall. There is absolutely *no way* that Satan could have tricked God and gained something that God would rather he not have!

Am I saying that God *wants* Satan to be "the god of this world?" Yes, for as long as it suits His divine purposes. If God didn't want Satan to operate, He would simply stop him, as we are told in Revelation 20:1-2 He will one day do.

I am not saying, however, that God wants *anyone* to remain under Satan's rule. God wants *everyone* to be saved and escape the domain of Satan (Acts 26:18; Col. 1:13; 1 Tim. 2:3-4; 2 Pet. 3:9). Yet God permits Satan to rule over everyone who loves darkness (Jn. 3:19)—those who continue in their rebellion against Him.

But isn't there anything we can do to help people escape Satan's dark kingdom? Yes, we can intercede for them and tell them the good news of Jesus Christ (as Jesus has commanded us). If they believe the gospel, they'll be delivered from Satan's authority. But to think that we can "pull down" the wicked spirits that hold people in their grasp is erroneous. If people want to stay in darkness, God will let them. Jesus told His disciples that if people in certain cities did not receive their message, they should shake the dust off their feet and go to another city (Matt 10:14). He did not tell them to stay and pull down the strongholds over the city so that the people would become more receptive. God allows wicked spirits to hold in bondage those who refuse to repent and turn to Him.

Further Proof of God's Supreme Authority Over Satan

There are many other scriptures which abundantly prove that God did not lose *any* control over Satan at the fall of man. The Bible repeatedly affirms that God always has had and always will have complete control over Satan. The devil can do only what God permits. Let's first examine some Old Testament illustrations of this fact.

The first two chapters of the book of Job include a classic example of God's authority over Satan. There we read of Satan, before the throne of God, accusing Job. Job was obeying God more than any other person on the earth at the time, and so naturally, Satan targeted him. God knew Satan had "set his heart" on Job (Job 1:8; see note in margin of NASB), and listened as Satan accused Job of serving God only because of all the blessings he enjoyed:

> Then Satan answered the Lord, "Does Job fear God for nothing? Hast Thou not made a hedge about him and his house and all that he has, on every side? Thou hast blessed the work of his hands, and his possessions have increased in the land. But put forth Thy hand now and touch all that he has; he will surely curse Thee to Thy face." Then the Lord said to Satan, "Behold, all that he has is in your power, only do not put forth your hand on him." So Satan departed from the presence of the Lord (Job 1:9-12).

Satan said that God had put a hedge around Job and requested that God take away Job's blessings. As a result, God permitted Satan to afflict Job *to a limited degree.* Initially, Satan could not touch Job's body. Later, however,

God did allow Satan to afflict Job's body, yet forbade Satan to kill him (Job 2:5-6).

This one passage of scripture clearly proves that Satan cannot do anything he wants. He couldn't touch Job's possessions until God permitted him. He couldn't steal Job's health until God permitted him. And he couldn't kill Job because God would not allow it.[2] God has control over Satan, even since the fall of Adam.

Saul's Evil Spirit "From the Lord"

There are several examples of God using Satan's evil spirits as agents of His wrath in the Old Testament. We read in 1 Samuel 16:14: "Now the Spirit of the Lord departed from Saul, and an evil spirit from the Lord terrorized him." This situation obviously occurred because of God's discipline upon disobedient King Saul.

The question is, what is meant by the phrase "an evil spirit from the Lord"? Does it mean that God sent an evil spirit who lived with Him in heaven, or does it mean that God sovereignly permitted one of Satan's evil spirits to afflict Saul? I think that most Christians would tend to accept more easily the second possibility in light of the rest of what the Bible teaches. The reason the scripture says that the evil spirit was "from God" was because that evil spirit's harassment was a direct result of God's divine discipline of Saul. Thus we see that evil spirits are under God's sovereign control.

In Judges 9:23 we read that "God sent an evil spirit between Abimelech and the men of Shechem," in order that divine judgment might come upon them for their wicked deeds. Again, this evil spirit was not from God's heaven, but from Satan's realm, and was divinely permitted to work evil plans against certain deserving persons. Evil spirits cannot successfully work their evil plans against anyone without God's permission. If that is not true, then

---

[2] This entire passage is also proof that Job did not "open the door to Satan through his fear" a myth believed by some. God Himself said to Satan concerning Job in 2:3: "And he [Job] still holds fast his integrity, although you incited Me against him, to ruin him without cause" (italics mine). I discuss this in detail in my book, God's Tests, pp. 175-181.

God is not all-powerful. Thus we can once more safely conclude that when Adam fell, Satan did not gain authority that was beyond God's control.

The Devourer of Malachi

In the final book of the Old Testament, God rebuked Israel for withholding their tithes and offerings, but promised that if they would repent, He would "rebuke the devourer" so that "it may not destroy the fruits of the ground; nor will your vine in the field cast its grapes" (Mal. 3:11).

Apparently, the Israelites were suffering crop failure as a result of "the devourer." Who was the devourer? No one can say with certainty, but it seems reasonable to suspect it was the devil or an evil spirit. If it was Satan or an evil spirit, then this indicates that God had the ability to put a stop to Satan's evil workings. The idea that God can't stop Satan because Satan got Adam's lease is once more proven untrue.

New Testament Examples of God's Power Over Satan

The New Testament provides additional evidence that refutes the Satan-Gained theory.

For example, we read in Luke 9:1 that Jesus gave His twelve disciples "authority over all the demons." Additionally, in Luke 10:19, Jesus told them, "Behold, I have given you authority to tread upon serpents and scorpions, and over *all the power of the enemy*, and nothing shall injure you" (italics mine).

It Jesus gave them authority over *all the power* of Satan, then He first must have had that authority Himself! Satan is under God's authority.

Later in Luke's gospel we read of Jesus saying to Peter, "Simon, Simon, behold, Satan has demanded *permission* to sift you like wheat..." (Luke 22:33). According to a note in the margin of my Bible, an alternate translation of the original Greek would read, "Satan has *obtained by asking* to sift you like wheat." Either way the text indicates that Satan could not sift Peter without first obtaining permission from God. Again, Satan is under God's control.

God Controls Temptations

Paul tells us in 1 Corinthians 10:13,

> No temptation has overtaken you but such as is common to man; and God is faithful, who will not allow you to be tempted beyond what you are able, but with the temptation will provide the way of escape also, that you may be able to endure it.

Here we are promised that God will not *allow* us to be tempted beyond what we are able. God controls the degree of temptation that we face. Therefore, He must have control over the tempter, Satan.

Satan's Thousand-Year Prison Term

When we read of the binding of Satan by one angel in Revelation 20, there is no mention of Adam's lease expiring. The reason given for his incarceration is simply "that he should not deceive the nations any longer" (Rev. 20:3).

Interestingly enough, after Satan is imprisoned for 1,000 years, he will be released and "will come out to deceive the nations which are in the four corners of the earth" (Rev. 20:8). Those deceived nations will then muster their armies to attack Jerusalem, where Jesus will be ruling. When they have surrounded the city, fire will come down from heaven and "devour them" (Rev. 20:9).

Would anyone be so foolish as to say that Adam's lease included one more short period of time after those 1,000 years, and so God was obligated to release Satan for that reason? I hope not!

No, what we learn once more from this section of Scripture is that God has complete control of the devil and permits him to work his deception only to fulfill His own divine purposes.

During the future 1,000 year rule of Jesus, Satan will be out of operation, unable to deceive anyone. There will be, however, people on the earth who are only outwardly obedient to Christ's rule, but who inwardly would love to see Him overthrown. Yet they will not attempt a coup knowing that they have no chance to overthrow the one who will "rule with a rod of iron" (Rev. 19:15).

But when Satan is released, he will be able to deceive those who, in their hearts, hate Christ, and they will foolishly attempt the impossible. As Satan is allowed to deceive potential rebels, the condition of people's hearts will be revealed, and then God can righteously judge those who are unfit to live in His kingdom.

That, of course, is one of the reasons God permits Satan to deceive people today. We will investigate God's purposes for Satan in a later chapter, but suffice it for now to say that God does not want anyone to *remain* deceived. He does, however, want to know what is in people's hearts. Satan cannot deceive those who know and believe the truth. But God allows the devil to deceive those who, because of their callous hearts, reject the truth.

Speaking of the time of the antichrist, Paul wrote;

> And then that lawless one will be revealed whom the Lord will slay with the breath of His mouth and bring to an end by the appearance of His coming; that is, the one whose coming is in accord with the activity of Satan, with all power and signs and false wonders, and *with all the deception of wickedness for those who perish, because they did not receive the love of the truth so as to be saved. And for this reason God will send upon them a deluding influence so that they might believe what is false, in order that they all may be judged who did not believe the truth, but took pleasure in wickedness* (2 Thes. 2:8-12; italics mine).

Notice that *God* is the one given the credit for sending a "deluding influence so that they might believe what is false." But also notice that these people who will be deluded are people who "did not believe the truth," indicating they had an opportunity, but still rejected the gospel. God will allow Satan to empower the antichrist with false signs and wonders so that Christ-rejecters will be deceived, and God's ultimate purpose is that "they may all be judged." For that same reason, God permits Satan to deceive people today.

If God had no reason to permit Satan to operate upon the earth, He could have easily banished him to some other place in the universe when he fell. We are told in 2 Peter 2:4 that there are certain sinful angels whom God has *already* cast into hell and committed "to pits of darkness, reserved for judgment." Our omnipotent God could have done the same thing to Satan and to any of his angels if it suited His divine purposes. But, for a while longer, God has good reasons to permit Satan and his angels to operate on the earth.[3]

The Demons' Fear of Torment

As we close our study of this particular myth, one final scriptural example to consider is the story of the Gadarene demoniacs:

> And when He [Jesus] had come to the other side into the country of the Gadarenes, two men who were demon-possessed met Him as they were coming out of the tombs; they were so exceedingly violent that no one could pass by that road. And behold, they cried out, saying, "What do we have to do with You, Son of God? *Have You come here to torment us before the time?*" (Matt. 8:28-29; italics mine).

Amazingly, this story is often used by the proponents of the Satan-Gained theory to support their doctrine. They say, "You see, those demons appealed to Jesus' justice. They knew He had no right to torment them before the time when Adam's lease expires, the time when they and Satan will be cast into the lake of fire to be tormented day

---

[3] Additional proof of God's sovereignty over Satan is found in Matthew 18:23-35, the parable of the unforgiving servant. Jesus concluded the parable by saying the the unforgiving servant was handed over to the torturers by his master until he should repay his debt. Then Christ warned, "So shall My heavenly Father also do to you, if each of you does not forgive his brother from your heart" (Matt. 18:35). Who are "the torturers"? It seems reasonable to conclude that they are evil spirits. We read in 1 Corinthians 5:5 Paul's instructions for disciplining a church-member by delivering him to "Satan for the destruction of his flesh." Here is another example of divine discipline though the agency of Satan.

and night forever (Rev. 20:10)."

But actually just the opposite is true. They knew Jesus had the power and every right to torment them any time He desired, which is why they begged Him for mercy. They obviously were very afraid that the Son of God might send them to torment much sooner. Luke tells us they entreated Him "not to command them to depart to the abyss" (Luke 8:31). If Jesus didn't have that right because of some supposed legal right of the devil, they wouldn't have been concerned at all.

Those demons knew they were completely at the mercy of Jesus, as illustrated by their plea not to be sent out of the country (Mark 5:10), their entreaty to be permitted to enter the nearby herd of pigs (Mark 5:12), their begging to not be cast into "the abyss" (Luke 8:31), and their imploring Christ not to be tormented before "the time."

Myth #3: "When Adam fell, Satan got Adam's lease to control the world."

No, Adam never had a lease to control the world. All he had was the authority to rule the animal kingdom. When he fell he didn't lose that authority. Satan gained nothing at the fall of Adam except a curse from God and a promise of his ultimate, complete demise. Satan was ruling over the kingdom of darkness before Adam was created, and when Adam sinned, he enrolled himself in Satan's already-existing kingdom. God always has and always will have total and complete authority over the devil. Jesus referred to His Father as "Lord of heaven and earth" (Matt. 11:25). Jesus said, "All authority has been given to Me in heaven and on earth" (Matt 28:18). He is, as Paul said, "the head over all rule and authority" (Col. 2:10).

MYTH #4:

"Satan, as 'the god of this world,' has control over everything on the earth, including human governments, natural disasters, and the weather."

Satan is spoken of in Scripture as being "the god of this world" by the apostle Paul (2 Cor. 4:4) and "the ruler of this world" by Jesus (Jn. 12:31; 14:30; 16:11). Based upon these titles for Satan, many have wrongly assumed that Satan has total control over the earth. Although the previous chapter contains enough scriptures to expose the error of this particular myth, it will do us well to study even further so that we can have a full understanding of just how limited Satan's power really is.

Before we begin, however, it would be helpful to interject some basic information about interpreting the Bible, because flawed interpretation is the most common reason for false belief.

A Foundational Rule

One of the most fundamental rules for interpreting the Bible (or interpreting any other book) is this: Read contextually. That is, we must not wrench isolated scriptures from the Bible to formulate our theology, but should read every sentence within the context of its surrounding sentences, paragraphs, chapters, and books. Let me offer you an obvious example of a violation of this rule.

I once heard a preacher give a sermon on the Christians' need to be "baptized in fire." He began his sermon by reading the words of John the Baptist from Matthew 3:11: "As for me, I baptize you with water for repentance, but He who is coming after me is mightier than I, and I am not fit to remove His sandals; He will baptize you with the Holy Spirit and fire."

Based upon this one verse, he built a sermon. I remember him saying, "Just because you are baptized in the Holy Spirit, that is not enough! Jesus also wants to baptize you in fire, just like John the Baptist proclaimed!" He went on to explain that, once we had been "baptized in fire," we would be full of zeal to work for the Lord. Finally he had an altar call for people who wanted to be baptized in fire.

Unfortunately, that particular preacher had made the classic mistake of taking a scripture out of its context.

What did John the Baptist mean when he said that Jesus would baptize with fire? To find the answer, all we need to do is read the two verses before that verse, and one verse after it. Let's begin with the two preceding verses. There John said:

> "And do not suppose that you can say to yourselves, 'We have Abraham for our father'; for I say to you, that God is able from these stones to raise up children to Abraham. And the axe is already laid at the root of the trees; every tree therefore that does not bear good fruit is cut down and *thrown into the fire*" (italics mine).

The first thing we learn is that at least part of John's audience that day consisted of Jews who thought their salvation was based upon their lineage. Thus, John's sermon was evangelistic.

The second thing we learn is that John was warning his listeners that unsaved people are in danger of being *cast into the fire*. It would seem reasonable to conclude that "the fire" of which John spoke in verse 10 is the same fire of which he spoke in verse 11!

This fact becomes even more clear when we read verse 12:

> "And His winnowing fork is in His hand, and He will thoroughly clear His threshing floor; and He will gather His wheat into the barn, *but He will burn up the chaff with unquenchable fire*" (italics mine).

In both verses 10 and 12, the fire of which John was speaking was the fire of hell. In verse 12, he metaphorically states that Jesus will divide people into two groups—wheat, which He will "gather into the barn," and chaff, which He will burn up "with unquenchable fire."

In light of the surrounding verses, John must mean in verse 11 that Jesus will baptize people *either* with the Holy Spirit, if they are believers, or with fire, if they are unbelievers. Since that is the case, no one should be preaching to Christians that they need to be baptized in fire!

Moving beyond the immediate context of these verses, we should also look to the rest of the New Testament. Can we find an example in the book of Acts where Christians are said to have been "baptized in fire"? No. Can we find an exhortation or any instruction in the epistles for Christians to be "baptized in fire"? No. Therefore, it is very safe to conclude that no Christian should be seeking a baptism in fire.

Back to "the god of this World"

I'm sure you see how vital it is that we interpret scriptures contextually. We must be cautious therefore, that our entire understanding of Satan is not built upon only three scriptures that refer to him as god, or ruler, of the world.

As we examine more of Scripture, we discover that not only did Jesus refer to Satan as "ruler of this world," but He also referred to His heavenly Father as "Lord of heaven *and earth*" (Matt. 11:25; Luke 10:21; italics mine). Additionally, not only did the apostle Paul refer to Satan as "the god of this world," but he, like Jesus, referred to God as "Lord of heaven *and earth*" (Acts 17:24; italics mine). This proves to us that neither Jesus or Paul would want us to think that Satan has complete control over the earth. Satan's authority must be limited.

A very important distinction between these contrasting scriptures is to be found in the words *world* and *earth*. Although we often use these two words synonymously in the English language, in the original Greek the two are usually not the same. Once we understand how they differ, our understanding of God and Satan's authority on the earth increases dramatically.

Jesus referred to God the Father as Lord of the *earth*. The word translated *earth* is the Greek word *ge*. It refers to the physical planet upon which we live, and from it our word *geography* is derived.

Contrariwise, Jesus said that Satan is the god of this *world*. The Greek word for *world* here is *kosmos*, and it refers primarily to order or arrangement. It speaks of *people* rather than of the physical planet itself. That is why we often speak of Satan as the "god of this world's *system*."

Presently, God does not have complete control over the *world*, because He does not have complete control over all the *people* of the world. The reason for this is that He has given all people a choice as to who will be their master, and many have chosen to give their allegiance to Satan. Humanity's free will, of course, is a part of God's plan.

Paul used a different word, *aion*, when he wrote of the god of this *world*. *Aion* can and often is translated as *age*, that is, a marked period of time. Satan is the god of this present age.

What does all this mean? The *earth* is the physical planet upon which we live. The *world* speaks of the people who presently live upon the earth, and more specifically, those who are not serving Jesus, but Satan, and who are caught up in his perverted, sinful system. We, as Christians, are said to be "in the world" but not "of the world" (John 17:11,14). We live among the citizens of the kingdom of darkness, but we are actually in the kingdom of light, the kingdom of God.

So now we have our answer. To put it simply: God is sovereignly in control of the entire earth. Satan, by God's permission, only has control of the "world's system," which is control of those who are citizens of his dark kingdom. For this reason, the apostle John wrote that the "whole *world* (not the whole *earth*) lies in the power of the evil one" (1 Jn. 5:19).

This is not to say that God has no authority over *the world*, or the world's *system*, or the people of the world. He is, as Daniel stated, "ruler over the realm of mankind, and bestows it on whomever He wishes" (Dan. 4:25). He still can exalt or humble any person He desires. However, as supreme "ruler over the realm of mankind," He has sovereignly permitted Satan to rule over the portion of mankind that is in rebellion against Him.

Satan's Offer Considered

This distinction between the earth and the world is also helpful in understanding Jesus' temptation in the wilderness. There Satan showed Jesus "all the kingdoms of the *world* in a moment's time." As I explained in the previous chapter, Satan could not have been offering Jesus a political position over earthly human governments, what we might call a president or premier. Satan is *not* the one who exalts and humbles earthly human rulers—God is. (This will be further proven later in this chapter.)

Rather, Satan must have shown Jesus all the sub-kingdoms of his world-wide kingdom of darkness. He showed Jesus the hierarchy of evil spirits who, in their respective territories, reign over the kingdom of darkness, as well as the rebel humans who are their subjects. Satan offered Jesus control over *his* domain—if Jesus would join Satan's rebellion against God. Jesus would then have become second-in-command over the kingdom of darkness.

This was designed by Satan as a temptation for power; then Jesus would have had control over every principality, power, world force of this darkness, spiritual force of wickedness in the heavenly places (Eph. 6:12), and every unsaved human. (This is, of course, all predicated upon the assumption that Satan was telling the truth.)

In summary, God has sovereign control and ownership of the earth and the world (see Psalm 24:1), but He has permitted Satan to have authority over "the world"—which consists of evil spirits and rebel human beings. This is what Jesus and Paul meant when they described Satan as the god or ruler of this world. Whether unsaved people realize it or not, their god is Satan. They believe his lies and serve him.

God's Control Over Earthly, Human Governments

The sacred cow we are trying to shoot in this chapter is the idea that Satan, as "ruler of this world" has control over everything on the earth, including human governments, natural disasters, and the weather. As we have more precisely defined Satan's title of "god of this world," however, we can see that Satan does not possess absolute control. Let's establish even more specifically the limits of Satan's authority by first examining scriptures that affirm God's authority over earthly, human governments. Satan has *some* authority in human governments only because he has some authority over unsaved people, and governments are often controlled by unsaved people. But ultimately, God is sovereign over human governments, and Satan can only manipulate them to the degree that God allows.

We have already examined, in the previous chapter, Daniel's statement to King Nebuchadnezzar, but because it is so illuminating, let us briefly consider it once more.

Great King Nebuchadnezzar was lifted up in pride because of his power and accomplishments, and so God decreed that he would be brought down to a low estate in order that he might learn that "the Most High is ruler over the realm of mankind, and bestows it on whom He wishes, and sets over it the lowliest of men" (Dan. 4:17). Obviously God deserved the credit for Nebuchadnezzar's rise to political greatness. This is true of every earthly leader. The apostle Paul, speaking of earthly rulers, declared that "there is no authority except from God, and those which exist are established by God" (Rom. 13:1).

God is the original and supreme authority of the entire universe. If anyone has any authority, it can only be because God delegated some of His or permitted someone to have some.

But what about evil rulers? Did Paul mean that even they are established by God? Yes he did. Earlier in the same letter, Paul wrote, "For the Scripture says to Pharaoh, 'For this very purpose I raised you up, to demonstrate My power in you, and that My name might be proclaimed throughout the whole earth'" (Rom. 9:17). God exalted hard-hearted Pharaoh for the purpose of glorifying Himself. God would show forth His great power though His delivering miracles—an opportunity afforded by a stubborn man whom He exalted.

Is this fact not also apparent in Jesus' conversation with Pilate? Amazed that Jesus would not answer his questions, Pilate said to Jesus, "You do not speak to me? Do You not know that I have authority to release You, and I have authority to crucify You?" (John 19:10).

Jesus replied, "You would have no authority over Me, *unless it had been given you from above...*" (John 19:11; italics mine). Knowing Pilate's cowardly character, God had exalted him in order that His preordained plan for Jesus to die on the cross would be consummated.

Just a cursory reading of the Old Testament books of history reveals that God sometimes uses evil human rulers as agents of His wrath upon deserving people. Nebuchadnezzar was used by God to bring God's judgment upon many Old Testament nations.

God Lifts Up and Brings Down

Consider also these three scriptures:

For not from the east, nor from the west, nor from the desert comes exaltation; but God is the Judge; *He puts down one, and exalts another* (Ps. 75:6-7; italics mine).

Daniel answered and said, "Let the name of God be blessed forever and ever, for wisdom and power belong to Him. And it is He who changes the times and the epochs; *He removes kings and establishes kings*; He gives wisdom to wise men, and knowledge to men of understanding" (Dan. 2:20-21; italics mine).

"He [God] has done mighty deeds with His arm; He has scattered those who were proud in the thoughts of their heart. *He has brought down rulers from their thrones*, and has exalted those who were humble" (Luke 1:51-52; italics mine).

There are numerous examples of rulers whom God exalted or brought down in the Bible. In the New Testament, we read of Herod, who failed to give glory to God when some of his subjects cried out before him, "The voice of a god and not of a man!" (Acts 12:22).

The result? "And immediately an angel of the Lord struck him...and he was eaten by worms and died" (Acts 12:23).

Keep in mind that Herod was definitely a citizen of Satan's kingdom, but he was not out of God's jurisdiction. Obviously, God could bring down any present earthly leader if He desired.[1]

---

[1] Does this mean that we should not pray for governmental leaders, or vote in elections, knowing that God exalts whoever He wants over us? No, in a democracy, God's wrath is practically built in. We get whom we vote for, and wicked people usually elect other wicked people. For this reason, the righteous should cast their vote. (And we should realize and thank God that He has allowed us to live under a democratic form of government. That in itself is an indication of His mercy upon us.) Additionally, in both Old and New Testaments, we are instructed to pray for our governmental leaders (Jer. 29:7; 1 Tim. 2:1-4), which indicates that we can influence God as He determines who will be put into office. Because God's judgment sometimes comes in the form of wicked governmental leaders, and because our nation is presently so deserving of judgment, we can ask for and obtain some mercy from Him, so that our county does not get everything it deserves.

God's Personal Testimony

Finally, let us read what God Himself once said through the prophet Jeremiah in regard to His sovereignty over earthly, human kingdoms.

> "Can I not, O house of Israel, deal with you as this potter does?" declares the Lord. "Behold, like the clay in the potter's hand, so are you in My hand, O house of Israel. At one moment I might speak concerning a nation or concerning a kingdom to uproot, to pull down, or to destroy it; if that nation against which I have spoken turns from its evil, I will relent concerning the calamity I planned to bring on it. Or at another moment I might speak concerning a nation or concerning a kingdom to build up or to plant it; if it does evil in My sight by not obeying My voice, then I will think better of the good with which I had promised to bless it" (Jer. 18:6-10).

Can you see that there is no way that Satan, when he tempted Jesus in the wilderness, could have been legitimately offering Jesus rule over earthly, human, political kingdoms? If he was telling the truth (as he sometimes does), then all he could have been offering Jesus was control over his kingdom of darkness.

But does Satan have *influence* in human governments? Yes, but only because he has influence over unsaved people, and unsaved people are involved in human governments. Yet he only has as much influence as God permits him to have, and God can foil any of Satan's schemes any time He desires. The apostle John wrote of Jesus as being "the ruler of the kings of the earth" (Rev. 1:5).

Does Satan Cause Natural Disasters and Adverse Weather?

Because Satan is "the god of this world," many have also assumed that he controls the weather and is the one who causes all natural disasters, such as droughts, floods, hurricanes, earthquakes and so on. But is this what Scripture teaches us? Again, we must be careful that we don't base our entire theology of Satan upon one scripture which says that "the thief comes only to steal, and kill, and destroy" (Jn. 10:10). How often I have heard people quote this verse as proof that anything that steals, kills, or destroys is from Satan. When we examine more of the Bible, however, we learn that God Himself sometimes kills and destroys. Consider these three examples out of many possible examples:

> There is only one Lawgiver and Judge, the One who is able to save and to *destroy*... (James 4:12; italics mine).

> But I will warn you whom to fear: fear the One who after He has *killed* has authority to cast into hell; yes, I tell you, fear Him! (Luke 12:5; italics mine.)

> "And do not fear those who kill the body, but are unable to kill the soul; but rather fear Him who is able to *destroy* both soul and body in hell" (Matt. 10:28; italics mine).

You can see that if we say that *everything* that involves killing or destroying is the work of Satan, we are mistaken. There are scores of examples of God killing and destroying in the Bible.

We should ask ourselves, *When Jesus spoke of the thief who comes to kill, steal, and destroy, was He actually speaking about the devil?* Again, all we need to do is read His statement contextually. One verse prior to His statement about the thief coming to kill, steal, and destroy, Jesus said, "All who came before Me are *thieves* and robbers, but the sheep did not hear them" (Jn. 10:8). When we read Jesus' entire discourse in John 10:1-15 stating He is the good Shepherd, it becomes even more obvious that His terms *thief* and *thieves* are references to false teachers and religious leaders.[2]

---

[2] This is not to say that Satan could not be described as a thief or as one who kills, steals, and destroys, or that false teachers are not motivated by Satan, but simply that, when Jesus made His statement about the thief in John 10:10, He was not thinking of Satan or evil spirits—He was thinking of false human teachers.

Various Views of Adverse Weather
and Natural Disasters

When a hurricane or earthquake strikes, it raises a theological question in the minds of people who believe in God: "Who is causing this?" There are only two possibilities for Bible-believing Christians: Either God or Satan causes them.

Some may object: "Oh no! God is not to blame! People are to blame. God is judging them for *their* sins."

I agree whole-heartedly. *If* God is *causing* hurricanes and earthquakes because of His judgment upon sin, then certainly we can lay the *blame* on rebel humans rather than on God, but still, God bears *responsibility*, as the natural disasters would not occur without His decree.

Or, if it is true that God *allows Satan* to send hurricanes and earthquakes to bring His judgment upon sinners, then we could say that *Satan* causes them, but still, God bears responsibility. The reason is because *He* is the one who permitted Satan to cause the destruction and because those disasters occur as a result of *His* reaction to sin.

Some say that neither God nor Satan are responsible for hurricanes and earthquakes, but that they are simply a "natural phenomena in our fallen world of sin." In a vague way, they are also attempting to lay the blame on humankind for natural disasters, but still missing the point. This explanation does not take God out of the picture. If hurricanes are simply a "natural phenomena in our fallen world of sin," who decided that they would be? Obviously hurricanes are not man-*made*. That is, hurricanes don't develop whenever a certain volume of lies are spoken into the atmosphere. Earthquakes don't occur when a certain number of people commit adultery.

No, if there is a relationship between hurricanes and sin, then God is involved, because hurricanes are a manifestation of His judgment upon sin. Even if they occur randomly, it would have to be God who decreed that they would occur randomly, and thus He is involved.

Even if there is *no* relationship between sin and natural

disasters, and God goofed when He designed the world, so that there are faults in the earth's crust that sometimes shift and weather systems that occasionally go berserk, still God would bear responsibility for earthquakes and hurricanes as He is the Creator, and His mistakes harm people.

No, Virginia, There is No "Mother Nature"

So we have only two possible answers for the question of natural disasters. Either God or Satan is responsible. Before we look at specific scriptures to determine which answer is correct, let's think further about those two possible answers.

If Satan is the one who causes natural disasters, then either God can or cannot stop Satan. If God *can* stop Satan from causing natural disasters but doesn't, then He again bears some responsibility. The disaster never would have occurred without His permission.

And now on the other side. Let's assume, for a moment, that God *can't* stop Satan, but He would like to. Is that really a possibility?

If God can't stop Satan from causing a natural disaster, then either Satan is more powerful than God, or Satan is smarter than God. This is, in effect, what adherents to the "Satan gained control over the world at Adam's fall" theory are saying. They claim that Satan has a legal right to do whatever he pleases on the earth because he stole Adam's lease. Now, supposedly, God would like to stop Satan but can't because He must honor Adam's lease which Satan now possesses. In other words, God was too stupid to foresee what would happen at the fall, but Satan, being more intelligent than God, has now gained power that God wishes he didn't have. Personally, I'm not about to say that Satan is more wise than God!

Hopefully, in the previous chapter, you have come to realize that the "Satan-Gained" theory is an unscriptural idea. If it were true, we would want to know why Satan doesn't cause more earthquakes and hurricanes than he presently does, and why he doesn't target large populations of Christians. (If you say "because God won't let him target populations of Christians," then you've just admitted that Satan cannot operate without God's permission!)

When we narrow it down specifically, the only two possible answers to our question are these: Either (1) God causes earthquakes and hurricanes or (2) Satan does *with God's permission*. There is no possibility that Satan causes them without God's permission, because that would be tantamount to saying that Satan is more powerful or more intelligent than God.

Can you see that regardless of which answer is correct, God is the one who is ultimately responsible? When people say, "God didn't send that hurricane—Satan did with God's permission," they are not totally letting God "off the hook" as they might hope. If God could have stopped Satan from causing the hurricane, regardless of whether He wanted to or not, then He bears responsibility. Rebel humans may be the ones to *blame* because of their sin (if the hurricane was sent by God or permitted by God as judgment), but still, it is foolish to say that God is in no way involved or responsible.

Scripture's Testimony

What, specifically, does Scripture say about "natural disasters"? Does the Bible say that God or the devil causes them? Let's look at earthquakes first because the Bible speaks of many.

According to Scripture, earthquakes might occur due to God's judgment upon deserving sinners. We read in Jeremiah: "At His [God's] wrath *the earth quakes*, and the nations cannot endure His indignation" (Jer. 10:10; italics mine).

Isaiah warns,

> From the Lord of hosts you will be punished with thunder and *earthquake* and loud noise, with whirlwind and tempest and the flame of a consuming fire (Is. 29:6; italics mine).

In this passage God is given the credit for the earthquake. *Perhaps* it occurred because God *allowed* Satan to cause it, but certainly no Christian, after reading this, could say that Satan, acting *independently* of God, sent this particular earthquake! If an earthquake is a manifestation of God's judgment, then God was involved.

You may recall that during the days of Moses, the earth opened up and swallowed Korah and his rebellious followers (see Num. 16:23-34). This was clearly an act of God's judgment. Other examples of God's judgment by earthquakes can be found in Ezek. 38:19; Ps. 18:7; 77:18; Hag. 2:6; Luke 21:11; Rev. 6:12; 8:5; 11:13; 16:18.

Some earthquakes that are recorded in Scripture are not necessarily acts of God's judgment, but nevertheless, were caused by God. For example, according to the gospel of Matthew, there was an earthquake when Jesus died (Matt. 27:51,54), and one when He was resurrected (Matt. 28:2). Did Satan cause those?

When Paul and Silas were singing praises to God at midnight in a Philippian jail, "suddenly there came a great *earthquake*, so that the foundations of the prison house were shaken; and immediately all the doors were opened, and everyone's chains were unfastened" (Acts 16:26; italics mine). Did Satan cause that earthquake? I don't think so. Even the jailer was saved after he witnessed God's power! And that is not the only God-caused earthquake in the book of Acts (see Acts 4:31).

I recently read of some well-meaning Christians who, upon hearing of a prediction of an earthquake in a certain area, traveled to the site to do "spiritual warfare" against the devil. Can you see the error in their assumption? It would have been scriptural for them to *pray* to *God* for *His mercy* upon the people who lived in that area. And if they had done that, there would have been no need to waste their time and money traveling to the potential earthquake site—they could have prayed to God right where they lived. But to battle the devil in order to stop an earthquake is unscriptural.

How About Hurricanes?

The word *hurricane* is not found in Scripture, but we can definitely find some examples of strong winds there. For example:

> Those who go down to the sea in ships, who do business on great waters; they have seen the works of the Lord, and His wonders in the deep. For *He spoke and raised up a stormy wind*, which lifted up the waves of the sea (Ps. 107:23-25; italics mine).

> And *the Lord hurled a great wind on the sea* and there was a great storm on the sea so that the ship was about to break up (Jonah 1:4; italics mine).

> After this I saw four angels standing at the four corners of the earth, holding back the four winds of the earth, so that no wind should blow on the earth or on the sea or on any tree (Rev. 7:1).

Obviously, God can start winds and stop them! Other scriptures which prove that God is in control of the wind are: Gen. 8:11; Ex. 10:13,19; 14:21; 15:10; Num. 11:31; Ps. 48:7; 78:76; 135:7; 147:18; 148:8; Is. 11:15; 27:8; Jer. 10:13; 51:16; Ezek. 13:11,13; Amos 4:9,13; Jonah 4:8; Hag. 2:17. In many of these examples, God used the wind as a means of judgment.

In all the Bible, there is only one scripture that gives Satan credit for sending a wind. It was during Job's trials, when a messenger reported to him: "A great wind came from across the wilderness and struck the four corners of the house, and it fell on the young people and they died" (Job 1:19).

We know from reading the first chapter of the book of Job that it was Satan who caused Job's misfortunes. We must not forget, however, that Satan could do nothing to harm Job or his children without God's permission. So, again, we see that God is sovereign over the wind.

The Gale on Galilee

What about the "fierce gale" that assailed Jesus and His

disciples when they were once boating across the Sea of Galilee? Surely it must have been Satan who caused that storm, as God would never send a wind that would capsize a boat that contained His own Son! "A kingdom divided against itself will fall," and so why would God ever send a wind that could potentially harm Jesus and the twelve disciples?

These are good arguments, but let us stop and think for a moment. If God didn't send the storm and Satan did, then we still must admit that God *allowed* Satan to send it. So the same question must still be answered: Why would God allow Satan to send a storm that might potentially harm Jesus and the twelve?

Is there an answer? Perhaps God was teaching the disciples something about faith. Perhaps He was testing them. Perhaps He was testing Jesus, who had to be "tempted in all things as we are, yet without sin" (Heb. 4:15). (To be fully tested, Jesus had to have an opportunity to be tempted to fear.) Perhaps God wanted to glorify Jesus. Perhaps He wanted to do all of the above.

God led the children of Israel to the edge of the Red Sea knowing full well they were trapped by Pharaoh's advancing army. But wasn't God *delivering* the Israelites? Then was He not working against Himself by leading them to a place where they would be massacred? Is this not an example of a "kingdom divided against itself"?

No, because God had no intention of letting the Israelites be massacred. And He had no intention, in sending *or* allowing Satan to cause a gale on the Sea of Galilee, of letting Jesus and the twelve be drowned.[3]

Regardless, the Bible doesn't say that Satan sent that gale on the Sea of Galilee, and it doesn't say God did either. Some say it had to be Satan because Jesus *rebuked* it. Perhaps, but that is not a water-tight argument. Jesus didn't rebuke *God*—He rebuked the wind. God the Father could have done the same thing. That is, He could have stirred up the wind with a word, and then calmed it by

[3] For further exploration of this often-neglected topic, see my book *God's Tests*.

rebuking it. Just because Jesus rebuked the gale is no proof that Satan caused it.

Again, we shouldn't base our entire theology on one verse that really proves nothing. I have already made reference to *scores* of scriptures that prove God is sovereignly in control of the wind, and He is most often given credit for sending it. My main point is that Satan, even though he is "god of this world," definitely does not have independent control over the wind or the right to cause a hurricane anytime or anywhere he desires.

Therefore, when a hurricane occurs, we should not view it as something that is beyond God's control, something He would like to stop but can't! Jesus' rebuke of the gale on the Sea of Galilee should be proof enough that God can stop a hurricane if He desires.

And if God is sending (or allowing) a hurricane, then He must have some reason, and the most intelligent answer why He would send or allow a storm that causes widespread *catastrophic* devastation is that He is warning and judging disobedient people.

"But Hurricanes Sometimes Harm Christians!"

But what about Christians who are affected by natural disasters? When a hurricane hits, it doesn't just demolish the homes of non-Christians. Aren't Christians exempt from God's wrath due to Jesus' sacrificial death? Then how can we say that God is the one ultimately behind natural disasters when they might very well harm His own children?

These are indeed difficult questions. We must realize, however, that the answers aren't any easier if we base them upon the false premise that Satan causes natural disasters. If Satan causes all natural disasters, then why does God *allow* him to cause things that might harm His own children? You see, we still face the same theological problem.

The Bible does state plainly that those who are in Christ are "not destined for wrath" (1 Thes. 5:9). At the same time, the Bible says that "the wrath of God abides on" those who don't obey Jesus (John 3:36). Yet how can God's wrath abide upon the unsaved without affecting the saved, when the saved live right among the unsaved? The answer is that, it often can't, and we should face up to that fact.

In the days of the exodus, all the Israelites were living together in one location, and the plagues which God sent as judgment upon the Egyptians did not harm them (see Ex. 8:22-23; 9:3-7; 24-26; 12:23). But with us, we live and work side-by-side with the "Egyptians." If God is to judge them by means of a natural disaster, then how are we to escape?

Escape is definitely the key word in understanding the answer to this question. Although Noah escaped God's full wrath when God flooded the earth, he still was adversely affected, as he had to labor to build the ark and then had to spend a year on board with a multitude of smelly animals! (Incidentally, both Old and New Testaments give *God* the credit for the flood of Noah, not Satan; see Gen. 6:17; 2 Pet. 2:5).

Lot escaped with his life when God's judgment fell upon Sodom and Gomorrah, but he still lost everything he had in the destruction of the fire and brimstone. God's judgment upon wicked people affected a righteous man.

Years in advance, Jesus had forewarned the believers in Jerusalem to flee when they saw their city surrounded by armies, because those would be "days of vengeance" (Luke 21:22-23)—clearly indicating God's wrathful purpose for allowing the Roman siege of Jerusalem in 70 A.D. Praise God that the Christians who heeded Christ's warning escaped with their lives, but they still lost what they had to leave behind in Jerusalem.

In all three of the above examples, we see that God's people may very well suffer to some degree when God's judgment falls upon the wicked. We cannot, therefore, jump to the conclusion that God is not responsible for natural disasters because they sometimes affect Christians.

But What About Babies and Children Who Suffer?

A similar argument that is used to prove that God is not in any way responsible for natural disasters is that children and babies are often affected adversely. But, again, that argument does not hold water according to the Bible. For example, when God flooded the earth in Noah's day, babies and children were drowned. That is just one of numerous biblical examples when God's judgment upon wicked people resulted in the deaths of innocent children.

But what alternative does God have when He judges evil people who also happen to be parents? Would it have been better for Joshua and the Israelites, rather than kill every man, woman, and child in the promised land as God commanded, to have spared the children and then raised them themselves? How would those children have reacted to being raised by the people who killed their parents? And at what age would the division be between those killed and those spared? You can see that if God destroys an entire wicked population of adults, such as He did in Sodom and Gomorrah, the children and babies are going to suffer— regardless of whether they live or die. The best alternative of those two terrible alternatives is that the children die. I'm convinced that any children under the so-called "age of accountability" would be immediately with the Lord at their deaths and be comforted and well taken care of in heaven.

We need to face up to the fact that it is impossible to punish parents without affecting their children. For example, when a father commits a crime and winds up in jail for five years, it affects his children. When that happens, as it does all the time, no one accuses the government of being unfair or cruel. No, the government is only fulfilling its duty to protect society from evil-doers. The person to blame for the child's suffering is the father who broke the law.

By the same token, when the moral Judge of the universe judges a parent and that judgment adversely affects his children, God is not the one to blame. In reality, the sinful acts of parents are exposed as even more sinful, as they know full well that because of their sins, their own innocent children might very well suffer consequences. When innocent children are harmed in a natural disaster, the evil adults are to blame, not God. My main point is that we cannot conclude that God is not responsible for natural disasters because those disasters affect children.

What Then Shall We Do?

We live in a world that is cursed by God, a world that is experiencing the wrath of God all the time. Paul wrote that "the wrath of God is revealed [not *going to be* revealed"] from heaven against all ungodliness and unrighteousness of men" (Rom. 1:18). As those who are living among an evil, God-cursed world, we cannot completely escape the effects of God's wrath upon it, even though that wrath is not aimed specifically at us.

Knowing this, what should we do? First, we should trust God. Jeremiah wrote:

> Blessed is the man who trusts in the Lord and whose trust is the Lord. For he will be like a tree planted by the water, that extends its roots by a stream and will not fear when the heat comes; but its leaves will be green, and it will not be anxious in a year of drought nor cease to yield fruit (Jer. 17:7-8).

Notice Jeremiah did not say that the man who trusts in the Lord will never be faced with a drought. No, when the heat and the famine come, the man who trusts in the Lord is like a tree that extends its roots by a stream. He has another source of supply, even while the world languishes around him. The story of Elisha being fed by ravens during the famine in Israel comes to mind as an example (see 1 Kings 17:1-6). David wrote of the righteous, "In the days of famine they will have abundance" (Ps. 37:19).

But aren't famines caused by the devil? No, not according to Scripture. God always takes the responsibility, and famine is often spoken of as a consequence of His wrath upon deserving people. For example:

Therefore, thus says the Lord of hosts, "Behold, *I am about to punish them*! The young men will die by the sword, *their sons and daughters will die by famine*" (Jer. 11:22; italics mine).

Thus says the Lord of hosts, "Behold, *I am sending* upon them the sword, *famine*, and pestilence, and I will make them like split-open figs that cannot be eaten due to rottenness" (Jer. 29:17; italics mine).

"Son of man, if a country sins against Me by committing unfaithfulness, and *I stretch out My hand against it, destroy its supply of bread, send famine against it*, and cut off from it both man and beast..." (Ezek. 14:13; italics mine).

"You look for much, but behold, it comes to little; when you bring it home, I blow it away. Why?" declares the Lord of hosts, "Because of My house which lies desolate, while each of you runs to his own house. Therefore, because of you the sky has withheld its dew, and the earth has withheld its produce. And *I called for a drought* on the land, on the mountains, on the grain, on the new wine, on the oil, on what the ground produces, on men, on cattle, and on all the labor of your hands" (Hag. 1:9-11; italics mine).

In the fourth example above, we read that the Israelites were given the blame for the drought because of their sin, but still, God claimed responsibility for sending it. For additional references to God causing famine, see Deut. 32:23-24; 2 Sam. 21:1; 24:12-13; 2 Kin. 8:1; Ps. 105:16; Is. 14:30; Jer. 14:12,15-16; 16:3-4; 24:10; 27:8; 34:17; 42:17; 44:12-13; Ezek. 5:12,16-17; 6:12; 12:16; 14:21; 36:29; Rev. 6:8; 18:8). Jesus Himself said that God "sends rain on the righteous and the unrighteous" (Matt. 5:45). God controls the rain.

If God sends a famine upon evil people, and we happen to live among those evil people, then we should trust that He will provide for our needs. Paul affirmed that famine cannot separate us from the love of Christ!: "Who shall separate us from the love of Christ? Shall tribulation, or distress, or persecution, or *famine*, or nakedness, or peril, or sword?" (Rom. 8:35; italics mine). Notice Paul did not say that Christians will never be faced with a famine, but rather implied that they might, even though he, as a student of the Scriptures, knew that famines can be sent by God to judge the wicked.

Obey and Insure

Second, we should be obedient and use godly wisdom to avoid being caught in any of God's wrath that is aimed at the world. Noah had to build his ark, Lot had to head for the hills, the Jerusalem Christians had to flee from their city; all of these had to obey God in order to avoid getting caught in His judgment upon the wicked.

If I lived in a hurricane zone, I'd make sure I had hurricane insurance. If I lived near a fault in the earth I'd either move or have earthquake insurance. And I'd pray. Every Christian should pray and remain sensitive to the One whom Jesus promised would "disclose to you what is to come" (John 16:13) so that he can avoid God's wrath upon the world.

We read in Acts 11 of the prophet Agabus who warned of an impending famine that could have been potentially disastrous to Christians living in Judea. Consequently, an offering was received by Paul and Barnabas for their relief (see Acts 11:28-30).

Can such things happen today? Certainly, because the Holy Spirit hasn't changed, nor has God's love waned. It is unfortunate, however, that some in the body of Christ are not open to such gifts and manifestations of the Holy Spirit, and thus, because they "quench the Spirit" (1 Thes. 5:19) miss out on some of God's best.

In his autobiography, the late president and founder of the Full Gospel Businessmen, Demos Shakarian, recounts how God spoke through an illiterate boy-prophet to the Christians living in Armenia in the late 1800's. He warned them of an impending holocaust, and as a result, thousands of pentecostal Christians who believed in such supernatural manifestations fled the country, including Shakarian's own grandparents. Shortly thereafter, a Turkish invasion of Armenia resulted in the slaughter of over a million Armenians, including those Christians who refused to heed God's warning.[4]

We would be wise to remain open to the Holy Spirit and be obedient to God, or else it is quite possible that we might experience a dose of God's wrath that He really doesn't want us to experience. Elisha once instructed a woman: "Arise and go with your household, and sojourn wherever you can sojourn; for the Lord has called for a famine, and it shall even come on the land for seven years" (2 Kin. 8:1). What if that woman hadn't listened to the prophet?

In the book of Revelation we read an interesting warning to God's people to come out of "Babylon" lest they be caught in God's judgment upon her:

> And I heard another voice from heaven, saying, "Come out of her [Babylon], my people, that you may not participate in her sins and *that you may not receive of her plagues*; for her sins have piled up as high as heaven, and God has remembered her iniquities....For this reason in one day her plagues will come, pestilence and mourning and famine, and she will be burned up with fire; for the Lord God who judges her is strong" (Rev. 18:4-5,8; italics mine).

In summary, God is sovereign over the weather and natural disasters. God has repeatedly proven Himself as Lord over nature in the Bible, from His causing forty days of rain during Noah's day, to His raining hailstones as well as sending other natural plagues upon Israel's enemies, to His stirring up the wind against Jonah's boat, to His rebuking the storm in the Sea of Galilee. He is, as Jesus said,

---

[4] There are, unfortunately, plenty of self-proclaimed prophets who are always predicting that California is going to slide into the ocean on a certain date, or some other such disaster. I wouldn't pay a bit of attention to any prophet unless he had a *proven* prophetic ministry with an accurate track-record, or unless God validated his ministry by some convincing accompanying sign, as He did in the case of the illiterate boy-prophet of whom Demos Shakarian wrote. See his book, *The Happiest People on Earth*, pp. 19-22 for the details.

"Lord of heaven and earth" (Matt. 11:25). For additional specific scriptural proof of God's lordship over nature, see Josh. 10:11; Job 38:22-38; Jer. 5:24; 10:13; 31:35; Ps. 78:45-49; 105:16; 107:33-37; 135:6-7; 147:7-8,15-18; Matt. 5:45; Acts 14:17.

Doesn't the Original Language Actually Say That God "Permitted" These Things?

A common explanation that is designed to "defend" God's loving character is that the original language of the Bible has been mistranslated. They would like us to believe that when the Bible states God "*sent* a famine," the Hebrew really says that He "*permitted* a famine" and so on.

Even if this were true, again, it really doesn't "let God off the hook" as some hope it will. If God *permits* a famine, then He obviously still bears some responsibility, as it could not have happened without His permission.

We need to wake up to the fact that we don't need to "let God off the hook." He is who He is, and He always acts in accordance with His perfect character. The real problem is that too many Christians do not understand God's character at all, thinking that He is all love and thus is never angered or wrathful. The fact is, however, that God is not only perfect in love, but also in holiness and justice and judgment, which are attributes that stem from His perfect love. The Bible is packed with examples of God's righteous wrath. In fact, unless we understand that God is wrathful, we cannot comprehend what Jesus did on the cross for us. Jesus paid the penalty for our sins, suffering the wrath of God that we deserved.

Have the many Hebrew and Greek verbs which speak of God's actions been mistranslated in the Bible? Does the ancient Hebrew or Greek language actually say that God did certain things in the permissive rather than causative sense? Actually, no, and if you ask any Hebrew or Greek language scholars those questions, they will give you the same answer. God unapologetically does what He does, and there is no need for us to try to make Him look better by claiming that He is really not responsible for certain things for which He claims responsibility! Additionally, even in cases when God *permits Satan* to bring harm to deserving people, God wants us to know that it isn't the devil who is punishing them, but He Himself. God is the holy one; Satan is the original sinner.

A Few Questions Answered

If God is judging people through famines, floods, and earthquakes, then is it wrong for us, as God's representatives, to assist and relieve the suffering of those whom God is punishing?

No, absolutely not. We should realize that God loves everyone, including people He judges. As strange as it may seem to our ears, His judgment through natural disasters is actually an indication of His love. How can that be? Through the hardship and difficulties that natural disasters cause, God is warning people whom He loves dearly that He is holy and judgmental, and that there is a consequence for sin. God allows temporal suffering in order to help people wake up to see their need for a Savior—in order that they might escape *eternal* suffering. That is love!

As long as people are still breathing, God is still showing them undeserved mercy and there is time for them to repent. Through our compassion and assistance, we can demonstrate God's love for people who are experiencing His temporal wrath, but who can be saved from His eternal wrath. Natural disasters are opportunities to reach out to the world for which Jesus died. I know of a church that won scores of people to Christ as they demonstrated His sacrificial love in practical ways during the aftermath of a hurricane.[5]

[5] And it seems that here in the United States, we have many opportunities to minister to people in the aftermath of natural disasters. Richard Hallgren, executive director of the American Meteorologist Society, says that "the United States has more severe weather and flooding than any other nation of the world." According to statistics gathered by the National Oceanic and Atmospheric Administration, in the average year "the United States can expect some 10,000 violent thunderstorms, 5,000 floods, more than 800 tornadoes and several hurricanes." (Source: *Why All the Crazy Weather?*, Reader's Digest, December, 1993, p. 96.) Is God sending the United States a message?

Isn't reaching people with the gospel the most important thing in this life? When we have an eternal perspective, the suffering of those caught in natural disasters is nothing in comparison to the suffering of those who will spend eternity in hell.

It is a fact the people generally become more receptive to the gospel when they are suffering. There are numerous biblical examples of this phenomena, from the repentance of Israel during the oppression of neighboring nations, to Jesus' story of the prodigal son. Christians should view natural disasters as times when the harvest is potentially very ripe.

Let's Tell the Truth

But what should our message be to those picking up the pieces of their lives after a hurricane or earthquake? How shall we answer if they ask for a theological answer to their predicament? We should tell them the truth, the truth found in the Bible, not someone's theory. Can you see how inconsistent our message sounds when we tell suffering people,

> "God did *not* send this hurricane, because God loves you. He would *never* send something that would cause so many people to suffer so much. He does, however, want you to repent of your sins and receive Jesus."

> "What will happen to me if I don't receive Jesus?"

> "God will to send you to hell where you and everyone like you will spend an eternity suffering as you burn in a lake of fire."

Why is it so difficult for us to believe that God would send a hurricane when we believe that He will incarcerate millions of people in hell to suffer forever?

Let's be honest with what the Bible teaches, and tell people that God is holy and that their sin does have consequences. Let's tell them that the ferocious roar of the hurricane is but a small sampling of the power that the almighty God possesses, and the fear they felt as their house shook is nothing in comparison to the terror that will grip them in hell. And let's tell them that even though we all deserve to spend eternity in hell, God so loved the world that He sent Jesus to pay the penalty for our sins on the cross, and through Him, we can be saved from God's wrath.

"But we shouldn't scare people about God, should we?" some ask. The answer is found in Scripture: "The fear of the Lord is the beginning of knowledge" (Prov. 1:7). Until people fear God, they really don't know anything.

I think that many of us have failed miserably in conveying the true gospel to the world around us.[6] God's judgment is falling around us everyday, and we tell people a lie about why such things happen—that it is the devil's work. And Oh how "the father of lies" loves for Christians to help him spread his lies!

What if People Become Angry With God?

But might not people become angry at God because of their suffering? Perhaps they will, but we gently need to help them see their pride. None have a right to complain at God for His treatment of them, because we all deserve to be in hell *right now*! Rather than cursing God for their calamity, people should be praising Him for loving them so much to warn them. God has every right to ignore everyone, leaving them to follow their selfish paths to hell. But God loves people and is calling out to them every day. He quietly screams at them through the flowering of apple trees, the songs of birds, the majesty of mountains, and the twinkling of a myriad of stars. He calls to them through His body, the church, and His Holy Spirit. But they ignore His call.

Certainly it is not God's will for people to have to suffer, but when they keep ignoring Him, He loves them enough to use more drastic measures to get their attention so that

---

[6] I have authored another book, titled *Christ's Incredible Cross*, that addresses the issue of the many unscriptural "gospels" that are proclaimed today.

they won't spend eternity in hell. Hurricanes, earthquakes, floods, and famines are some of those more drastic measures.

Is God Unfair in His Judgment?

When we look at God and our world from a biblical perspective, then and only then are we thinking rightly. The biblical perspective is that everyone deserves to be in hell right now, but that God is merciful. When suffering people say they deserve better treatment from God, surely He must groan!

Once we understand God's perspective, we no longer question His fairness. Everyone is receiving much more mercy than he or she deserves. The person whose home has been destroyed in an earthquake has no right to be angry at God. He should be thanking God that he is still alive. Those whose homes are still standing should be twice as thankful for the even greater mercy they've been shown!

In keeping with this theme, Jesus once commented on two contemporary calamities. We read in Luke's gospel:

> Now on the same occasion there were some present who reported to Him [Jesus] about the Galileans, whose blood Pilate had mingled with their sacrifices. And He answered and said to them, "Do you suppose that these Galileans were greater sinners than all other Galileans, because they suffered this fate? I tell you, no, but unless you repent, you will all likewise perish. Or do you suppose that those eighteen on whom the tower in Siloam fell and killed them, were worse culprits than all the men who live in Jerusalem? I tell you, no, but unless you repent, you will all likewise perish" (Luke 13:1-5).

The Galileans who died at Pilate's hand could not say, "God has treated us unfairly by not saving us from Pilate!" No, they were sinners who deserved to die. And, according to Jesus, those Galileans who survived would be wrong to jump to the conclusion that they were less sinful than their murdered neighbors. They had not *earned* greater favor from God—they had been *granted* greater mercy.

Christ's message was clear: "You are *all* sinners. Sin has consequences. For now, you live because of God's mercy. So repent before it is too late for you as well."

Jesus concluded His comments on those tragedies with a parable about God's mercy:

> And He began telling this parable: "A certain man had a fig tree which had been planted in his vineyard; and he came looking for fruit on it, and did not find any. And he said to the vineyard-keeper, 'Behold, for three years I have come looking for fruit on this fig tree without finding any. Cut it down! Why does it even use up the ground?' And he answered and said to him, 'Let it alone, sir, for this year too, until I dig around it and put in fertilizer; and if it bears fruit next year, fine; but if not, cut it down'" (Luke 13:6-9).

Here are the justice and mercy of God illustrated. God's justice cries out, "Cut down the worthless tree!" But His mercy pleads, "No, give it more time to bring forth fruit." Every person who is without Christ is like that tree.

Can We Rebuke Hurricanes and Floods?

One final question about natural disasters. Is it not true that if we have enough faith, we can rebuke and stop natural disasters from occurring?

To have faith means to believe God's revealed will. Faith, therefore, must be founded upon God's own Word, or it is not faith at all, but rather hope or presumption. There is no place in the Bible where God gives us the promise that we can rebuke and calm hurricanes, and so there is no way a person could have faith to do so.

Let me explain further. The only way a person could have *faith* to rebuke a hurricane is if he was *certain* God did not want that hurricane to strike a certain geographical area. As we have learned from Scripture, God is the one who controls the wind and is thus responsible for hurricanes. Therefore, it would be impossible for someone to have confident faith that he could stop a hurricane when God Himself has decreed its occurrence. The only exception to this would be if God changed His mind about the hurricane, which He might do in response to someone's prayer that He show mercy, or in response to the repentance of the people whom He was about to judge (the story of Nineveh in Jonah's day comes to mind as an example). Yet even if God changed His mind, still no one could have faith to rebuke and calm a hurricane unless that person *knew* God had changed His mind and also knew that God wanted him to rebuke and calm the storm.

The only person who ever rebuked and calmed a great wind was Jesus. The only way any of us could do it would be if God gave us the "gift of faith," (or the gift of "special faith" as it is sometimes called), one of the nine gifts of the Spirit listed in 1 Corinthians 12:7-11. As with all the gifts of the Spirit, the gift of faith operates not as we might will, but only as the Spirit wills (1 Cor. 12:11). Therefore, unless God gives you special faith to rebuke an oncoming hurricane, you should not remain in its path, supposedly acting in faith. You should get out of the way! I would also suggest that you pray for God's protection, and ask Him to have mercy upon the people He was judging, asking Him to spare their lives that they might have more time to repent.

Notice that when Paul was bound for Rome on a boat that was driven for two weeks by gale-force winds, he did not calm it by a rebuke (see Acts 27:14-44). The reason he didn't is because he couldn't. Also notice that God did have mercy upon every person on board, as all 276 of them survived the resulting shipwreck (see Acts 27:24,34,44). I would *like* to think that God had mercy upon them because Paul prayed for God to have mercy on them.

Myth #4:"Satan, as 'the god of this world' has control over everything on the earth, including human governments, natural disasters, and the weather."

No, God, who is "Lord of heaven and earth," has sovereign control over the entire universe and earth, including human governments, natural disasters, and the weather. Satan only has God's permission to rule over the kingdom of darkness, which includes evil spirits upon the earth and unsaved human beings. As soon as a person receives Christ as Lord and Savior, he is taken out of Satan's kingdom and authority and placed into God's kingdom, because on the cross, Jesus paid the penalty for our sin and broke Satan's power over us.

MYTH #5:

"We can pull down demonic strongholds in the atmosphere through spiritual warfare."

There is no doubt, according to Scripture, that Satan rules over a hierarchy of evil spirits who inhabit the earth's atmosphere and who assist him in ruling the kingdom of darkness. That those evil spirits are "territorial," ruling over certain geographical areas, is a concept that is also contained in the Bible (see Dan. 10:13, 20-21; Mark 5:9-10). That Christians have the authority to cast demons out of other people and the responsibility to resist the devil is scriptural (see Mark 16:17; Jas. 4:7; 1 Pet. 5:8-9). But can Christians pull down evil spirits over cities? The answer is that they can't, and to attempt to do so is a waste of their time.

Before we expose the error of this particular myth, it would be helpful for us once again to consider another common-sense rule of sound Bible interpretation. Let's begin by looking at an example of some Christians in the Bible who misinterpreted, because of an assumption, a statement Jesus once made. Our example is found in John's gospel, and occurred after Jesus' resurrection.

Upon learning from Jesus about future persecution he himself would suffer, Peter questioned the Lord about his fellow disciple, John:

> Peter therefore seeing him [John] said to Jesus, "Lord, and what about this man?" Jesus said to him, "If I want him to remain until I come, what is that to you? You follow Me!" This saying therefore went out among the brethren that that disciple would not die; yet Jesus did not say to him that he would not die, but only, "If I want him to remain until I come, what is that to you?" (John 21:23-21).

Here is a classic example of some Christians who misinterpreted Jesus' words because they read into His statement more than He intended. Jesus never said that John would not die; He only said that if He wanted John to be alive at His return, it was His own business, and none of Peter's!

I'm sure you can see how it would have been tempting to read into Jesus' words and assume that John would not die. But we must be careful that we don't make a similar error when we interpret *any* of God's Word. We must be cautious in making any assumption that cannot be clearly proven from what the Bible says, or else we could find ourselves believing something that is not true.

This kind of misinterpretation is often made, however, by many Christians. Just because we can cast demons out of people, we should not assume that we can pull down evil spirits over cities. There are numerous examples of casting demons out of people in the gospels and the book of Acts, but can you think of even one example in the gospels or the book of Acts where someone pulled down an evil spirit that was ruling over a city or geographical area? You can't because there are no such examples. Can you think of one instruction anywhere in the epistles about our responsibility to pull down evil spirits from the atmosphere? No, because there are none. For this reason, we have no biblical basis to believe that we can or should be waging "spiritual warfare" against evil spirits in the atmosphere.

Extrabiblical or Unbiblical?

Errors of assumption are often justified by the argument, "I may not be able to prove what I am doing is correct according to the Bible, but you can't prove that it is incorrect either." Claiming that there is vast difference between what is *unbiblical* and what is *extrabiblical*, they justify their practice, classifying it as not necessarily supported by Scripture, yet not refuted by Scripture either.

This is a weak argument indeed. If God wants us to know something or do something, He makes it quite clear in Scripture. Why would anyone want to practice a kind of spiritual warfare for which there is no instruction or example in the Bible? Why not rather practice that which is clearly revealed as God's will in Scripture, such as casting demons out of people, preaching the gospel, making disciples, and praying scripturally?

Moreover, as we study Scripture closely, that which may be classed by some as extrabiblical is often exposed as being very unbiblical. Such is the case with the concept of pulling down territorial spirits.

Pushing Parables Too Far

Reading more meaning into the Bible than God intended is an error Christians often make when they read scripture passages containing metaphorical language. The Bible is full of comparisons, because they help us understand spiritual concepts. When Jesus said, "the kingdom of heaven is like...," He took something His listeners did understand to explain something they did not understand. Metaphors are extremely helpful in aiding the learning process.

We must not forget, however, that every comparison is imperfect, because the two things compared are not usually identical in every respect. A metaphor is defined as a comparison of things *basically unlike* but having *some* striking similarities. For this reason, we must be cautious that we do not force a meaning upon a metaphor that God never intended. For example, Jesus once said:

> "The kingdom of heaven *is like* a dragnet cast into the sea, and gathering fish of every kind; and when it was filled, they drew it up on the beach; and they sat down, and gathered the good fish into containers, but the bad they threw away (Matt. 13:47-48; italics mine).

What did Jesus mean in this comparison? Like most of His parables, He wanted to convey one point. In this case, He wanted us to know that not everyone will automatically get into the kingdom of heaven, but that there will be a separation into two categories, good and bad. But that is where the similarities between His story of the gathered fish and the kingdom of heaven end.

Certainly Jesus was not trying to teach us that the kingdom of heaven will consist of fish! Or that the good fish in heaven will be put into containers! Or, if you are smart enough to realize that the fish in the story represent people, Jesus does not want us to think that those people are going to be caught in a big dragnet or that their judgment before God will take place on a beach! Moreover, Jesus was not trying to teach us, as "good fish," that our salvation is earned by our good works. Any of these conclusions would be reading more into His parable than He intended.

Yet how often this is done by some who try to read meaning into every minor detail of Jesus' more lengthy and detailed parables. They end up confused, because they fail to realize that in every comparison, at some point, similarities turn to dissimilarities.

Because Scripture so often contains metaphorical language, we must be careful that we don't fall into that trap, as unfortunately, many who teach about spiritual warfare have done. Satan is a master at twisting Scripture (see Matt. 4:5-7). He loves it when we misinterpret what God says.

"Pulling Down Strongholds"

The Bible does sometimes use military terminology when describing the Christian's responsibility. Yet, in those cases, we must ask ourselves if we are "pushing the parables too far," by reading more into metaphorical language than was meant. For example, a classic text that is often misinterpreted is 2 Corinthians 10:3-6:

> For though we walk in the flesh, we do not war according to the flesh, for the weapons of our warfare are not of the flesh, but divinely powerful for the destruction of fortresses. We are destroying speculations and every lofty thing raised up against the knowledge of God, and we are taking every thought captive to the obedience of Christ, and we are ready to punish all disobedience, whenever your obedience is complete (2 Cor. 10:3-6).

The *King James Version*, rather than saying "we are destroying speculations," says we are "pulling down strongholds." From this one metaphorical phrase, practically an entire theology has been built to defend the idea of doing "spiritual warfare" in order to "pull down the strongholds" consisting of evil spirits in the atmosphere. But as the *New American Standard Version* clearly conveys, Paul is speaking, not of evil spirits in the atmosphere, but of strongholds of false beliefs that exist in people's minds. *Speculations* are what Paul was destroying, not wicked spirits in high places.

This becomes even more clear as we read contextually. Paul said, "We are destroying speculations and every lofty thing raised up against *the knowledge of God*, and we are taking every *thought* captive to the obedience of Christ" (italics mine). The battle of which Paul symbolically writes is a battle against thoughts, or ideas that are contrary to the true knowledge of God.

Using military metaphors, Paul explains that we are in a battle, a battle for the minds of people who have believed the lies of Satan. Our primary weapon in this battle is the truth, which is why we've been commanded to go into all the world and preach the gospel, invading enemy territory with a message that can set captives free. The fortresses we are destroying have been built with building blocks of lies, joined by the mortar of deception.

If you will take the time to read all of the tenth chapter of Paul's second letter to the Corinthians, you will see that he makes no mention there of wicked spiritual powers, even though we know (and he knew) that wicked spirits are involved in spreading lies. Therefore, in this particular passage, evil spirits were not the "strongholds" of which he was thinking when he wrote. To say that Paul's words in 2 Corinthians 10:3-6 prove that we can and should practice pulling down evil spirits in the atmosphere is an obvious misrepresentation of what Paul actually meant. If Paul did mean that we should pull down evil spirits in the atmosphere, we would have to wonder why he himself never practiced what he preached, as there is no mention of him ever doing it in the history of his ministry as recorded in the book of Acts.

The Whole Armor of God

Another passage in Paul's writings that is often misinterpreted is found in his Ephesian letter:

> Finally, be strong in the Lord, and in the strength of His might. Put on the full armor of God, that you may be able to stand firm against the schemes of the devil. For our struggle is not against flesh and blood, but against the rulers, against the powers, against the world forces of this darkness, against the spiritual forces of wickedness in the heavenly places. Therefore, take up the full armor of God, that you may be able to resist in the evil day, and having done everything, to stand firm. Stand firm therefore, having girded your loins with truth, and having put on the breastplate of righteousness, and having shod your feet with the preparation of the gospel of peace; in addition to all, taking up the shield of faith with which

you will be able to extinguish all the flaming missiles of the evil one. And take the helmet of salvation, and the sword of the Spirit, which is the word of God (Eph. 6:10-17).

May I initially point out that although this passage is definitely about the Christian's struggle with the devil and evil spirits, there is no mention of pulling down evil spirits over cities. As we study the passage closely, it becomes clear that Paul is primarily writing about each individual's responsibility to resist Satan's schemes *in his personal life* by applying the truth of God's Word.

Notice also the evident metaphorical language of the entire passage. Paul obviously was not speaking of a literal, material armor that Christians should put on their bodies. Rather, the armor of which he speaks is figurative. Those pieces of armor represent the various scriptural truths that Christians should use for protection against the devil and evil spirits. By knowing, believing, and acting upon God's Word, Christians are, figuratively speaking, clothed in God's protective armor.

Let's examine this passage in Ephesians verse by verse, while asking ourselves, *What was Paul really trying to convey to us?*

The Source of Our Spiritual Strength

First, we are told to "be strong in the Lord, and in the strength of His might" (Eph. 6:10). The emphasis is on the fact that we should *not* derive our strength from ourselves but God. This is further brought out in Paul's next state- ment: "Put on the full armor of God..." (Eph. 6:11a). This is God's armor, not ours. Paul is not saying that God Himself wears armor, but that we need the armor which God has supplied for us.

Why do we need this armor which God has supplied? The answer is, "that you may be able to stand firm against the schemes of the devil" (Eph. 6:11b). That is the reason. This armor is primarily for *defensive*, not offensive use. It is not so we can go out and pull down evil spirits over cities; it is so we can *stand firm against* Satan's schemes!

We learn that the devil has evil plans to attack us, and unless we are wearing the armor that God supplies, we are vulnerable. Notice also that it is *our* responsibility to put on the armor, not God's.

Let's continue:

> For our struggle is not against flesh and blood, but against the rulers, against the powers, against the world forces of this darkness, against the spiritual forces of wickedness in the heavenly places (Eph. 6:12).

Here it becomes crystal clear that Paul is not talking about a physical, material battle, but a spiritual one. We are struggling against the schemes of various ranks of evil spirits whom Paul lists. Most Bible students assume that Paul listed those evil spirits as they are ranked from bottom to top, "rulers" being the lowest class and "spiritual forces of wickedness in the heavenly places" being the highest class.

How can we struggle against spiritual beings? That question can be answered by asking, *How can spiritual beings attack us?* They attack us primarily with temptations, thoughts, suggestions, and ideas that contradict God's Word and will. Therefore, our defense is knowing, believing, and obeying God's Word.

> "Therefore, take up the full armor of God, that you may be able to resist in the evil day, and having done everything, to stand firm" (Eph. 6:13).

Notice, once again, that Paul's purpose is to equip us to *stand* against Satan's attacks. His purpose is not to equip us to go out and attack Satan and pull down evil spirits from the atmosphere. Three times in this passage Paul tells us to *stand firm.* Our position is one of defense, not offense.

This is not to say that we never take an offensive stand, but that this passage is primarily speaking of maintaining a strong defense. When we proclaim the gospel, for example, we are definitely "invading enemy territory" in an offensive measure.

Also, notice once again that it is our responsibility to take up the armor and to stand firm. *God will not do it for us.*

Truth—Our Primary Defense

Stand firm therefore, having girded your loins with truth...(Eph. 6:14a).

Here is what keeps our armor in place—the truth. What is the truth? Jesus said to His Father, "Thy word is truth" (John 17:17). We cannot successfully stand firm against Satan unless we know the truth with which we can counter his lies. Jesus beautifully demonstrated this during His temptation in the wilderness as He responded to Satan's every suggestion with, "It is written..."

Paul continued:

"...and having put on the breastplate of righteousness...(Eph. 6:14b).

One of Satan's most successful schemes is to condemn Christians. He is called "the accuser of our brethren" in Scripture (see Rev. 12:10), and when we sin, he would like us to believe that we have forfeited our salvation and that there is no hope.

Praise God, however, that "there is therefore now no condemnation for those who are in Christ Jesus" (Rom. 8:1). Because we are in Christ, the One who paid the full penalty for our sins, we no longer have to fear being condemned by God. God may *convict* us of sin, but He will not *condemn* us as He will those who are not in Christ. We have become "the righteousness of God" in Christ (2 Cor. 5:21). That means that through Christ, we have been declared "not guilty"! Knowing and believing that we are righteous is like having on a breastplate that protects our hearts from accepting Satan's condemnation.

Firm Footing in Gospel Shoes

"...and having shod your feet with the preparation of

the gospel of peace..." (Eph. 6:15)

Knowing, believing and acting upon the truth of *the gospel* gives us firm footing to stand against Satan's attacks. The shoes that Roman soldiers wore had long spikes on the bottom that gave them a firm grip on the battlefield. When we know that Jesus has died for our sins and been raised from the dead for our justification, Satan's lies are unable to knock us off our feet.

Paul specifically refers here to "the gospel of peace." We now have "peace with God through our Lord Jesus Christ" (Rom. 5:1). This gives us confidence to stand firm against Satan's lies that God is still angry with us, or that we will go to hell when we die, or that God will not answer our prayers. We have peace with God.

> "...in addition to all, taking up the shield of faith with which you will be able to extinguish all the flaming missiles of the evil one (Eph. 6:16).

Notice again Paul's emphasis here on our defensive posture. He is not talking about our pulling down demons over cities. He is talking about our using faith in God's Word to resist the devil's lies. When we believe and act upon what God has said, it is like having a shield that protects us from Satan's lies, represented figuratively as the "flaming missiles of the evil one."

Our Spiritual Sword—God's Word

> "And take the helmet of salvation, and the sword of the Spirit, which is the word of God" (Eph. 6:17).

Salvation, as the Bible describes it, includes our deliverance from Satan's captivity. God has "delivered us from the domain of darkness, and transferred us to the kingdom of His beloved Son" (Col. 1:13). Knowing this is like having a helmet that guards our minds from believing Satan's lie that we are still under his dominion. Satan is no longer our master—Jesus is.

Additionally, we are to take "the sword of the Spirit" which, as Paul explains, is figurative for the Word of God.

As I already mentioned, Jesus was the perfect example of a spiritual warrior who skillfully yielded His spiritual sword. During His temptation in the wilderness He responded to Satan each time by quoting directly from God's Word. So too, if we are to defeat the devil in spiritual combat, we must know and believe what God has said, lest we fall for his lies.

Also notice that Jesus used "the sword of the Spirit" *defensively*. Some like to point out, to those of us who maintain that the armor of which Paul wrote is primarily defensive, that a sword is definitely an offensive weapon. Thus, with a very weak argument, they try to justify their theory that this passage in Ephesians 6:10-12 is applicable to our supposed responsibility to offensively "pull down strongholds" of evil spirits in the heavenly places.

Obviously, from reading Paul's own reason why Christians should put on God's armor (that they may "stand firm against the schemes of the devil"), we know that he is speaking primarily of a defensive use of the armor. Additionally, although a sword can be thought of as an offensive weapon, it can also be thought of as defensive, as it blocks and protects from the thrusts of the opponent's sword.

Moreover, we must be careful that we don't strain the entire metaphor, as we attempt to wrench from the armor pieces significance that really doesn't exist. When we begin to argue about the defensive and offensive nature of a sword, we are very likely "pushing the parable too far" as we carve into pieces a simple metaphor that was never meant to be so dissected.

Most importantly, notice that every piece of the armor which Paul described relates somehow to the truth of the Word of God. Knowing, believing, and acting upon God's Word are the ways we overcome Satan's schemes against us.

Didn't Jesus Instruct Us to "Bind the Strong Man"?

Three times in the gospels we find Jesus making mention of "binding the strong man." In none of those three cases, however, did He tell His followers that "binding the strong man" was something they should practice. Let's examine exactly what Jesus did say, and let's read what He said contextually:

> And the scribes who came down from Jerusalem were saying, "He is possessed by Beelzebul," and "He casts out the demons by the ruler of the demons." And He called them to Himself and began speaking to them in parables, "How can Satan cast out Satan? And if a kingdom is divided against itself, that kingdom cannot stand. And if a house is divided against itself, that house will not be able to stand. And if Satan has risen up against himself and is divided, he cannot stand, but he is finished! *But no one can enter the strong man's house and plunder his property unless he first binds the strong man, and then he will plunder his house.* Truly I say to you, all sins shall be forgiven the sons of men, and whatever blasphemies they utter; but whoever blasphemes against the Holy Spirit never has forgiveness, but is guilty of an eternal sin"—because they were saying, "He has an unclean spirit" (Mark 3:23-30; italics mine).

Notice that Jesus was not teaching His followers to bind any strong men. Rather, He was responding to the criticism of the Jerusalem scribes with unassailable logic and a clear metaphor.

They accused Him of casting out demons by using demonic power. He responded by saying that Satan would be insane to work against himself. No one can intelligently argue with that.

If it wasn't Satan's power that Jesus used to cast out demons, then whose power was He using? It had to be a power stronger than Satan's. It had to be God's power, the power of the Holy Spirit. Thus Jesus spoke metaphorically of Satan, comparing him to a strong man guarding his possessions. The only one able to take the strong man's possessions would be someone even stronger, namely, Himself. This was the true explanation as to how He cast out demons.

Satan is the "strong man," and Jesus is the one who overpowered him to plunder his house. Isn't that exactly what Jesus did through His sacrificial death? He broke Satan's power over all those who would believe in Jesus. His casting out of demons was a foreshadowing of an even greater deliverance that He would accomplish for Satan's captives!

Jesus concluded by warning those scribes of the great danger they were in by attributing to Satan the work of the Holy Spirit.

This passage that mentions the strong man, as well as the similar ones found in Matthew and Luke, cannot be used to justify our "binding strong men" over cities. Additionally, when we examine the rest of the New Testament, we do not find any examples of anyone "binding strong men" over cities, or any instruction for anyone to do so. We can thus safely conclude that it is unscriptural for any Christian to attempt to bind and render powerless some supposed "strong man-evil spirit" over a city or geographic area.

What About "Binding on Earth and in Heaven"?

Only twice in the gospels do we find Jesus' words, "Whatever you shall bind on earth shall be [or 'have been'] bound in heaven, and whatever you shall loose on earth shall be [or 'have been'] loosed in heaven." Both instances are recorded in Matthew's gospel.

Was Jesus teaching us that we can and should "bind" demonic spirits in the atmosphere?

First, let's consider His words, *binding* and *loosing*. Jesus' use of those words is *obviously* metaphorical, as He certainly did not mean that His followers would be taking physical ropes or cords and literally binding anything or literally loosing anything that was bound with physical ropes or cords. Jesus must have used the words *binding* and *loosing* figuratively. What did He mean?

For the answer, we should look at His use of the words *binding* and *loosing* within the context of whatever He was speaking of at the time. Was He talking on the subject of evil spirits? If so, we could conclude that His words about binding have application to the binding of evil spirits.

Let's examine the first passage where Jesus mentioned binding and loosing:

> He [Jesus] said to them, "But who do you say that I am?" And Simon Peter answered and said, "Thou art the Christ, the Son of the living God." And Jesus answered and said to him, "Blessed are you, Simon Barjona, because flesh and blood did not reveal this to you, but My Father who is in heaven. And I also say to you that you are Peter, and upon this rock I will build My church; and the gates of Hades shall not overpower it. I will give you the keys of the kingdom of heaven; and *whatever you shall bind on earth shall have been bound in heaven, and whatever you shall loose on earth shall have been loosed in heaven.* (Matt. 16:15-19; italics mine).

No doubt the reason this passage has been interpreted in so many ways is that it contains at least five metaphorical expressions: "flesh and blood," "rock," "gates of Hades," "keys of the kingdom of heaven," and "binding/loosing." All of these expressions are figurative, speaking of something else.

Hades' Gates

Regardless of the precise meaning of the metaphors, you can see that, in this passage, Jesus did not mention evil spirits. The closest He came was His mention of the "gates of Hades," which are, of course, symbolic, as there is no way that the literal gates of Hades could do anything to hinder the church.

What do the "gates of Hades" represent? Perhaps they are symbolic of Satan's power, and Jesus meant that Satan's power would not stop His church from being built. The Bible, however, really doesn't associate Satan's power with Hades (or hell) as we often do. Satan is not presently living in Hades or ruling in hell as He often is portrayed in cartoons. The Scripture teaches that his domain is primarily the realm of the earth. Satan will *one day* be cast into the lake of fire, but it won't be so that he can rule there, but so that he can be tormented there day and night! (see Rev. 20:10). Shortly after Satan is cast into the lake of fire, Hades itself will be cast there as well (see Rev. 20:14). So, again, the "gates of Hades" are not a likely symbolism for Satan's power or authority.

More likely, what Jesus meant by His statement is that the church He would build would save people from the eternal fate of being imprisoned behind Hades' gates. Those terrible gates, which forever hold captive people who died without Christ, will have fewer to constrain because of Christ's saving work on the cross and because of His church being built.

Notice that Jesus actually makes reference to two sets of gates: the gates of Hades, and the gates to heaven, implied by His giving Peter the "keys to heaven." This contrast further supports that idea that Jesus' statement about Hades' gates is representative of the church's role in saving people from going to Hades. Keep in mind that it was not Satan who constructed gates into Hades, it was God.

Nevertheless, even if Jesus did mean that "all the power of Satan would not stop His church," we cannot jump to the conclusion that His comments about binding and loosing are instructions as to what we should be doing with evil spirits over cities, for the simple reason that we can find no examples in the gospels or Acts of anyone binding evil spirits over cities, nor can we find any instructions in the epistles for doing such a thing. However we interpret Christ's words about binding and loosing, our interpretation must be supported *contextually within the rest of the New Testament*. In light of the absence of *any* scriptural example, it is amazing how often we say such things as, "I bind the devil in Jesus name," or "I loose the angels over that person," or I loose God's mercy in that situation" and so on. You don't find anyone saying such things anywhere in the New Testament. The emphasis in Acts and the epistles is not on speaking to the devil or binding and loosing evil spirits, but on preaching the gospel and praying to God. For example, when Paul was being continually buffeted by a messenger (literally, "angel") of Satan, he didn't try to "bind" it. He prayed to God about it (see 2 Cor. 12:7-10).

The Keys to Heaven

Let's look further at the immediate context of Jesus' words about binding and loosing. Note that directly before He mentioned binding and loosing, Jesus said that He would give Peter the "keys to the kingdom of heaven." Peter was never given any literal keys to heaven's gates, and so Jesus' words must be taken as metaphorical. What do "keys" represent? Keys represent *the means of access to something that is locked.* One who has the keys has means that others do not have to open certain doors.

As we consider Peter's ministry as reported in the book of Acts, what is it that we find him doing that could be considered comparable to opening doors that are locked to others?

Primarily, we find him proclaiming the gospel, the gospel which opens heaven's doors for all who will believe (and the gospel which shuts the gates of Hades). In that sense, all of us who are Christ's followers possess the "keys to the kingdom of heaven," as we all can and should share the good news that can open the door of heaven to anyone. *The keys to the kingdom of heaven can only be the gospel of Jesus Christ.* It wasn't until after Jesus was resurrected that Peter understood that Jesus had died for the sins of the world on the cross, and only then did he have a gospel to proclaim that could open heaven's doors.

And Now, Binding and Loosing

Finally, after promising to give Peter the keys to the kingdom of heaven, Jesus made His statement about binding and loosing, His fifth metaphorical expression in the passage under consideration.

Within the context of the statements we have already examined, what did Jesus mean? How does Peter's binding and loosing have application to Jesus building His church, to the saving of people from Hades, and to proclaiming the gospel?

I can think of only two possibilities as to what the expression, *binding and loosing* represents, one being a more strict interpretation and the other being less strict.

First the more strict: Perhaps Jesus meant that if Peter didn't use the keys to the kingdom by proclaiming the gospel, people would remain bound by Satan. But, if Peter did proclaim the gospel, people would be loosed from Satan's grasp.

Jesus wanted to impress upon Peter (and us) that we have been given a great responsibility. No one can be saved unless *we* preach the gospel (see Rom. 10:14). *We* hold the keys to the kingdom of heaven. It is our responsibility to spread the gospel—the *only* message that can open heaven's doors (and close Hades' gates). God won't open (or shut) those doors without us. *We have the keys.*

In keeping with this same theme, Jesus said to Peter that whatever *he* would bind would be bound in heaven, and whatever *he* would loose would be loosed in heaven. The responsibility of binding and loosing falls upon us, not upon God in heaven. Heaven will back us up, but we are God's *only* messengers of a gospel that can set people free.

This interpretation of Jesus' words fits well with the context of the rest of Scripture. We don't find anyone binding demons over cities or over anything else in the book of Acts, but we do find Christ's followers taking very seriously their responsibility to proclaim a gospel that sets people free from Satan.

If we don't share the gospel, leaving people bound by Satan, God will leave them bound. If, however, we do share the gospel, a gospel that, if believed, looses people from sin and Satan, God in heaven will loose them.

But if that is what Jesus meant, why didn't He just say it that way? I don't know! But the fact is, Jesus often used powerful figures of speech to provoke us to think and to make His points unforgettable. In order to convey to us how much we should love God, He once told us to hate our fathers, mothers, and children (see Luke 14:26). To communicate how terrible a place hell will be, He told us to pluck out our eyes and cut off our hands in order to escape it (see Matt. 18:8-9).

A Similar Statement

In a declaration that is similar to His statement about binding and loosing, we once find Jesus saying to His disciples, "If you forgive the sins of any, their sins have been forgiven them; if you retain the sins of any, they have been retained" (John 20:23).

Obviously, Jesus did not mean that His disciples had the authority to forgive or not forgive anyone's sins. Only God has that authority, and we don't find the apostles forgiving or retaining anyone's sins in the book of Acts.

We do find them, however, proclaiming a message that offers people the forgiveness of their sins. We have the God-given right to tell anyone who believes the gospel that his sins are forgiven. And we have the God-given right to tell anyone who rejects the gospel that his sins are not forgiven.

That must be what Jesus meant, but *notice how He said it*. We are not forgiving people of their sins, but are proclaiming a message that can bring them God's forgiveness. We are not binding or loosing anyone, but we are proclaiming a message that will either loose people from sin and Satan or leave them bound.

A Less Strict Interpretation

The other, less strict interpretation finds less significance in the metaphorical words, *binding* and *loosing*. Perhaps all that Jesus meant was, "I'm authorizing you as heaven's representative. Fulfill your responsibility on earth, and heaven will back you up."

If an employer said to his salesman, "Whatever you do in Omaha will be done in the home office," how would that salesman interpret his boss's words? He would take them to mean that he was authorized to represent his company in Omaha. Perhaps all that Jesus meant was that we who are His on earth are authorized to represent Him who is in heaven.

This less strict interpretation of Jesus' words harmonizes well with His second use of the same expression, found two chapters after the first passage in Matthew's gospel:

> "And if your brother sins, go and reprove him in private; if he listens to you, you have won your brother. But if he does not listen to you, take one or two more with you, so that by the mouth of two or three witnesses every fact may be confirmed. And if he refuses to listen to them, tell it to the church; and if he refuses to listen even to the church, let him be to you as a Gentile and a tax-gatherer. Truly I say to you, *whatever you shall bind on earth shall be bound in heaven; and whatever you loose on earth shall be loosed in heaven.* Again I say to you, that if two of you agree on earth about anything that they may ask, it shall be done for them by My Father who is in heaven. For where two or three have gathered together in My name, there I am in their midst" (Matt. 18:15-20; italics mine).

In this second passage that mentions binding and loosing, there is absolutely *nothing* within the text that would lead us to believe that Jesus was speaking of binding evil spirits. Here Christ spoke of binding and loosing directly after speaking on the subject of church discipline.

This would seem to indicate that in reference to binding and loosing in this passage, Jesus meant something like, "I'm giving *you* responsibility to determine who should be in the church and who should not. It is your job. As you fulfill your responsibilities, heaven will back you up."

In a broader application, Jesus was saying, "You are authorized on earth as heaven's representatives. You have responsibilities, and as you fulfill your responsibilities on earth, heaven will always support you."

Binding and Loosing in Context

This interpretation fits well within the immediate context as well as the wider context of the rest of the New Testament.

In regard to the immediate context, we note that directly after His statement about binding and loosing, Jesus said: "Again I say to you, that if two of you agree *on earth* about anything that they may ask, it shall be done for them by My Father who is *in heaven*" (Matt. 18:19; italics).

There again is the theme of "what you do on earth will be supported in heaven." We on earth are authorized and responsible to pray. When we do, heaven will respond. Jesus' words, "*Again* I say..." seem to indicate He is expanding upon His prior statement about binding and loosing.

Jesus' final statement in this passage, "For where two or three have gathered together in My name, there I am in their midst," also supports the "heaven will back you up as you act" theme. First believers must gather; then Jesus will be in their midst.

The Church Has Responsibilities

The general idea conveyed in the passage is that the church has responsibility. The church has a responsibility to determine who should, and who should not be accepted as a member. It has the responsibility to pray. It has responsibility to gather together. The church should never have an attitude of "whatever will be, will be," or think that God's will is automatically done regardless of what we do. No, we have God-given responsibility. When we do what God has told us to do, He will support us.

As we consider the wider context of all the New Testament, we find this interpretation abundantly supported. We find the church fulfilling certain responsibilities and heaven backing her up. We find the Christians gathering, and then Jesus being in their midst by His Holy Spirit. We find them not accepting everything that happens as God's will, agreeing in prayer together that certain circumstances would change, and God answering their prayer. We find them disciplining those within the church, not waiting for God to do what He has told them to do. In fact, Paul once wrote concerning the discipline of a church member in Corinth,

> I wrote you in my letter not to associate with immoral people; I did not at all mean with the immoral people of this world, or with the covetous and swindlers, or with idolaters; for then you would have to go out of the world. But actually, I wrote to you not to associate with any so-called brother if he should be an immoral person, or covetous, or an idolater, or a reviler, or a drunkard, or a swindler—not even to eat with such a one. For what have I to do with judging outsiders? *Do you not judge those who are within the church? But those who are outside, God judges. Remove the wicked man from among yourselves* (1 Cor. 5:9-13; italics mine).

Notice Paul indicated it was the church's responsibility to excommunicate a false brother, not God's.

As we consider both of the passages that mention binding and loosing, and if we assume that in both, the meaning of the binding and loosing expression is the same, then it seems the best interpretation for what Jesus meant is the less strict one: "You are My ambassadors, My authorized representatives. Do your job, and heaven will support you."

Even if you totally disagree with my interpretation of the passages in consideration, you are going to be hard pressed to present a sound, scriptural argument that Jesus was speaking about binding evil spirits over cities![1]

---

[1] One final question that could be asked about that particular interpretation is this: If Jesus meant that we are to bind evil spirits, did He also mean that sometimes we should loose evil spirits? If not, then what are we supposed to loose? Some might claim we should loose God's power, or loose His angels, or loose His protection, and so on, as some Christians often attempt to do. But where in the New Testament can we find anyone doing such things?

God's Divine Plan Includes Satan

Satan and his angels are a rebel army, but not an army that is beyond God's control. This rebel army was *created by God*, (although they were not rebellious when first created). Paul wrote:

> For by Him [Christ] all things were created, both *in the heavens* and on earth, visible and *invisible*, whether *thrones or dominions or rulers or authorities*—all things have been created by Him and for Him (Col. 1:16; italics mine).

Jesus created every angelic spirit of every rank, including Satan. Did He know that some would rebel? Of course He did. God is all-knowing. Then why did He create them? Because He would use those rebel spirits to help fulfill His plan. If He had no purpose for them, He would simply have incarcerated them, as we are told He has already done with some rebellious angels (2 Pet. 2:4) and as He will one day do with Satan (Rev. 20:2).

My point is that God has reasons for allowing Satan and every evil spirit to operate upon the earth. If He didn't, they would be completely out of commission. What are God's reasons for allowing Satan to operate upon the earth? I don't think anyone understands every reason, yet God has revealed some of the reasons in His Word.

First, God allows Satan to operate limitedly on the earth to fulfill His plan to test humans. Satan serves as the alternate choice for humanity's allegiance. Whether they realize it or not, people are in subjection either to God or Satan. God permitted Satan to tempt Adam and Eve, two people who possessed God-given free wills, in order to test them. All those with free wills must be tested to reveal what is in their hearts, either obedience or disobedience.[2]

Second, God allows Satan to operate limitedly on the earth as an agent of His wrath upon evil doers. I have already proven this in a previous chapter by several specific cases in Scripture when God brought judgment

---

[2] This concept is discussed much more thoroughly in my book, *God's Tests*.

upon deserving people through evil spirits. Just the fact that God has allowed Satan to rule over the unsaved people of the world is an indication of His wrath upon them. God judges groups of evil people by allowing wicked humans to rule over them, and also by allowing wicked spiritual beings to rule over them, making their lives all the more miserable.

Third, God allows Satan to operate limitedly on the earth to glorify Himself. "The Son of God appeared for this purpose, that He might destroy the works of the devil" (1 John 3:8). Every time God destroys one of Satan's works, it glorifies His power and wisdom.

Presently, it is God's will that Satan and evil spirits operate upon the earth. This is not to say that God wants anyone to remain under Satan's dominion or be oppressed by evil spirits. He wants them all to be saved and be free. But as long as there are people who are in rebellion against Him, God will continue to use Satan and evil spirits to fulfill His plans. For this reason, it is foolish to think that we can bind territorial spirits from operating on the earth.

Jesus is the Head Over Principalities and Powers

As Christians, our scriptural responsibility to deal with Satan and evil spirits is two-fold: to resist them in our own lives (Jas. 4:7), and to cast them out of others who want to be delivered (Mark 16:17). Any Christian who has experience in casting demons out of other people knows that, as a general rule, unless the demonized person wants to be delivered, he will be unable to cast the demon out.[3] God honors every person's free will, and if a person wants to yield to evil spirits, God won't stop him.

This is yet another reason why we can't pull down territorial spirits over geographic areas. Those evil spirits are there holding people in bondage because that is what those people have chosen. Through proclaiming the gos-

---

[3] The exception to this rule would be in cases of people who are so controlled by demons that they have no way of communicating their desire for freedom. In those cases, special gifts of the Spirit would be necessary to bring deliverance, and gifts of the Spirit operate as the Spirit wills.

pel to them, we offer them a choice. If they make the right choice, it will result in their freedom from Satan and evil spirits. But if they make the wrong choice, choosing not to repent, God will allow Satan to hold them captive.

Jesus is spoken of in Scripture as being "the head over all rule and authority" (Col. 2:10). Although the Greek words for *rule* (arche) and *authority* (exousia) are sometimes used in describing human political leaders, they are also used in the New Testament as titles for demonic spiritual rulers. The classic passage about the Christians struggle against rulers (arche) and powers (exousia) in Ephesians 6:12 is one example.

When we read contextually what Paul wrote about Jesus being the head over all rule and authority in Colossians 2:10, it seems clear that he is speaking of spiritual powers. For example, in the same passage just four verses later, Paul writes of Jesus, "When He had disarmed the *rulers* and *authorities*, He made a public display of them, having triumphed over them through Him" (Col. 2:15).

If Jesus is the head of the spiritual rulers and authorities, then He is sovereign over them. This is a wonderful revelation to Christians living in pagan, animistic cultures, who spent their former lives worshipping idols in fear of the evil spirits whom they knew ruled over them. To those of us living in "enlightened" cultures, where it is thought that evil spirits do not actually exist, the revelation of Christ's headship over spiritual rulers and authorities is not so exciting. But it should be, once we discover that we, just like those in more primitive societies, were living in captivity to evil spirits.

The Only Way of Escape

The only way to escape the captivity of evil spirits is to repent and believe the gospel. That is the escape God has provided. No one can bind the demonic forces over a city and set you free or set you partially free. Until a person repents and believes the gospel, He is abiding in God's wrath (John 3:36), which includes being held by demonic powers.

That is why there are no measurable changes in the cities where the big spiritual warfare conferences and sessions have taken place, because nothing has happened that has really affected the demonic hierarchies that rule in those areas. Christians can scream at principalities and powers all day and night; they can attempt to torment the devil by so-called "warring tongues"; they can say "I bind you evil spirits over this city" a million times; they can even do all these things up in airplanes and on the top floors of skyscrapers (as some actually do); and the only way the evil spirits will be affected is that they will get a good laugh at the foolish Christians.

This is a good place to conclude this chapter and prepare to launch into examining the next myth, the myth that we can open the door for effective evangelism by doing spiritual warfare against territorial spirits.

Myth #5: "We can pull down demonic strongholds in the atmosphere through spiritual warfare."

No, we can't. God created them and allows them to remain there, and they will be there until it no longer suits His divine purposes. God could do away with all of them right now if He desired. There is no example of anyone pulling down any territorial spirits in the New Testament; neither are there any instructions found there for Christians to do so.

MYTH #6:

"Spiritual warfare against territorial spirits opens the door for effective evangelism."

The driving motivation for many Christians who are heavily involved in doing spiritual warfare against territorial spirits is their desire to see God's kingdom expanded. For this they are to be commended. Every Christian should desire to see more people escape from Satan's grasp and an eternity in hell.

It is important, however, that we use God's methods to build God's kingdom. God knows what works and what is a waste of time. He has told us exactly what our responsibilities are in regard to the expansion of His kingdom. To think we can do something not found in Scripture that will multiply the effectiveness of our evangelism, something that Jesus, Peter, or Paul never practiced in their ministries, is foolish.

Why do so many Christians think that spiritual warfare can open the door to effective evangelism? Their line of reasoning usually sounds something like this: "Satan has blinded the minds of unsaved people. We must therefore do spiritual warfare against Satan to stop him from blinding them. Once the blinders are removed, more people will believe the gospel." Is this true?

There is certainly no doubt that Satan has blinded the minds of unsaved people. Paul wrote:

> And even if our gospel is veiled, it is veiled to those who are perishing, in whose case the god of this world has blinded the minds of the unbelieving, that they might not see the light of the gospel of the glory of Christ, who is the image of God (2 Cor. 4:3-4).

The question before us is, *Did Paul give this piece of information to the Corinthian Christians with the intent of motivating them to do spiritual warfare and pull down territorial spirits?*

The answer is *No* for several obvious reasons.

First, because Paul did not go on to say, "Therefore Corinthians, because Satan has blinded the minds of unbelievers, I want you to do spiritual warfare and pull down territorial spirits so those blinders will be removed." Rather, the very next thing he mentioned was his preaching of Christ (which is the way that spiritual blindness *is* removed).

Second, in *none* of his letters did Paul instruct any believers to be involved in pulling down strongholds over their cities that evangelistic results might increase.

Third, we know from reading all of Paul's letters that he did not believe Satan's blinding was the *primary* reason why unbelievers remained unbelieving. Satan's blinding is a contributing factor, but not the main or only factor. *The primary factor that keeps people unsaved is the hardness of their hearts*. This is obvious for the simple reason that Satan is not able to keep everyone blinded. Some people, when they hear the truth, believe it, and thus reject any lies they formerly believed. It is not so much Satan's blinding that causes their unbelief, as it is their unbelief that allows Satan's blinding.

Callous Hearts

In his letter to the Ephesians, the apostle Paul explained precisely why non-Christians remain in unbelief:

> This I say therefore, and affirm together with the Lord, that you walk no longer just as the Gentiles also walk, in the futility of their mind, being *darkened in their understanding* [perhaps a reference to Satan's blinding], excluded from the life of God, because of the ignorance that is in them, *because of the hardness of their heart*; and they, having become *callous*, have given themselves over to sensuality, for the practice of every kind of impurity with greediness (Eph. 4:17-19; italics mine).

Paul said that the unsaved are excluded from the life of God because of "the ignorance that is in them." But why are they ignorant? Why has their "understanding been darkened"? The answer is, "because of the hardness of their hearts." They have become "callous." That is the root and primary reason why people remain unsaved.[1] They bear the blame themselves. Satan only supplies the lies they want to believe.

Jesus' parable of the sower and the soils illustrates this concept perfectly:

> "The sower went out to sow his seed; and as he sowed, some fell beside the road; and it was trampled under foot, and the birds of the air ate it up....Now the parable is this: the seed is the word of God. And those beside the road are those who have heard; then the devil comes and takes away the word from their heart, so that they may not believe and be saved" (Luke 8:5, 11-12).

Notice that the seed, which represents the gospel, fell beside the road and was trampled. It couldn't penetrate the hard soil where people frequently walked. Thus is was

---

[1] Paul's description of unbelievers in Romans 1:18-32 also supports this same concept.

easy for birds, which represent the devil, to steal the seeds.

The point of the entire parable is to compare the condition of people's hearts (and their receptivity to God's Word) with various types of soil. Jesus was explaining why some people believe and why others do not: It all depends upon them.

How does Satan figure into the picture? He is only able to steal the Word from those with hardened hearts. The birds in the parable were only a secondary cause as to why the seeds did not germinate. The primary problem was with the soil; in fact, it was the soil's hardness that made it possible for the birds to get the seeds.

The same thing is true with the gospel. The real problem is with the hardened hearts of free moral agents. When people reject the gospel, they make a choice to remain blinded. They would prefer to believe lies rather than the truth. As Jesus put it, "The light is come into the world, and *men loved the darkness* rather than the light; for their deeds were evil" (John 3:19; italics mine).

The Bible does not lead us to believe that people are sincere, good-hearted folks, who would surely believe the gospel if Satan would only stop blinding them. On the contrary, the Bible paints a very dim picture of human character, and God will hold every individual responsible for his sinful choices. Sitting on His throne of judgment, God will not accept anyone's excuse that "the devil made me do it."

How Satan Blinds People's Minds

Exactly how does Satan blind people's minds? Does he possess some mystical spiritual power that he pours like a potion into people's heads to dull their understanding? Does a demon dig its talons into their brains, effectively short-circuiting their rational thinking processes? No, Satan blinds people's minds *by supplying them with lies to believe.*

Obviously, if people really believed the truth that Jesus is the Son of God who died for their sins, if they really believed that they will one day have to stand before Him to give an account of their lives, then they would repent and become His followers. But they don't believe those things. They do, however, believe *something*. They may believe that there is no God, or that there is no life after death. They may believe in reincarnation, or that God would never send anyone to hell. They may think that their good works will get them into heaven. But whatever they believe, if it is not the gospel, it can be summed up in one word: *lies*. They don't believe the truth, and thus Satan keeps them blinded through lies. If, however, they decide to believe the truth, Satan will be able to blind them no longer.

The Lies of Darkness

Satan's kingdom is referred to in Scripture as the "kingdom of *darkness*." Darkness, of course, represents the absence of truth, the absence of light. When you are in darkness, you navigate by your imagination, and usually end up stubbing your toe on a bedpost! That is how it is in Satan's kingdom of darkness. Those who are in it are navigating their lives by their imaginations, and their imaginations have been filled with Satan's lies. They are in spiritual darkness.

Satan's kingdom is best defined then, not as a geographical kingdom with clearly defined borders, but as a kingdom of belief—belief, that is, in lies. The kingdom of darkness is located in the same place as the kingdom of light. Those who believe the truth live right among those who believe lies.[2] Our primary job is to proclaim the truth to people who already believe lies. When someone believes the truth, Satan loses another one of his subjects because he is no longer able to deceive him.

Thus we set unsaved people free from Satan, not by "binding" evil spirits over them but by proclaiming the truth. Jesus said, "You shall know the truth, and *the truth shall make you free*" (John 8:32; italics mine). Spiritual

---

[2] It is true, of course, that in various geographical areas, there are greater or lesser percentages of people in either kingdom.

blindness is removed by truth.

Within that same passage of Scripture in John's gospel, Jesus said to an unsaved audience:

> "You are of your father the devil, and you want to do the desires of your father. He was a murderer from the beginning, and *does not stand in the truth, because there is no truth in him. Whenever he speaks a lie, he speaks from his own nature; for he is a liar, and the father of lies.* But because I speak the truth, you do not believe Me (John 8:44-45).

Notice the contrast Jesus made between Himself and the devil. He spoke the truth; Satan is the ultimate liar.

Notice also that even though Jesus told His listeners that they were of their father the devil, and even though He exposed Satan as a liar, He still placed responsibility on them to believe the truth He spoke. It was not the devil's fault that they were blinded—it was their own fault. Jesus held them responsible. Satan assists people who "love darkness" to stay in the darkness by supplying them with lies to believe. But Satan can't fool anyone who will believe the truth.

The primary way we can push back the kingdom of darkness is by spreading the light—the truth of God's Word. That is why Jesus did *not* tell us, "Go into all the world and bind the devil," but rather, "Go into all the world and preach the gospel." Jesus told Paul that the purpose of his preaching would be to open people's "eyes *so that they may turn* from darkness to light and from the dominion of Satan to God..." (Acts 26:18; italics mine). This makes it clear that people escape Satan's dominion when they are exposed to the truth of the gospel and then make a decision to turn from darkness to light, that is, believe the truth rather than a lie. The only strongholds we are "pulling down" are strongholds of lies built in people's minds.

This is God's Plan

Don't forget that God is the one who cast Satan out of heaven to the earth. He could have put Satan anywhere in the universe or incarcerated him forever. But He didn't. Why? Because God wanted to use Satan to accomplish His ultimate goal—the goal one day to have a big family of free moral agents who would love Him, having chosen to serve Him.

If God wanted a family of children that would love Him, then two things were required. First, He had to create people with free wills, because the foundation of love is free will. Robots can't love.

Second, He had to test them in an environment where they would be faced with a choice to obey or disobey, to love or hate Him. Free moral agents *must* be tested. And if there is going to be a test of loyalty, there must exist a temptation to disloyalty. Thus, we begin to understand why God placed Satan on the earth. Satan would serve as the alternate choice for humanity's allegiance. He would be permitted (with certain limitations) to influence anyone who was receptive to his lies. Thus everyone would be faced with the choice: *Will I believe God or Satan? Will I serve God or Satan?* Whether people realize it or not, they have all made a decision already. Our job is to encourage people who have made the wrong decision to repent and believe the gospel.

Is this not what happened in the garden of Eden? God placed the tree of the knowledge of good and evil there and then forbade Adam and Eve to eat from it. If God didn't want them to eat from it, why did He place it there? The answer is that it served as a test.

We also note that Satan was permitted by God to tempt Eve. Again, if loyalty is to be tested, there must exist the temptation to be disloyal. Satan lied to Eve and she believed him, and so, at the same time, she decided *not* to believe what God had said. The result? The first free moral agents revealed the disloyalty that was in their hearts.

In a similar manner, every free moral agent is tested throughout his or her lifetime. God has revealed Himself through His creation, and so everyone can see that there is an awesome God who exists (Rom. 1:19-20). God has given every one of us a conscience, and in our hearts, we know right from wrong (Rom. 2:14-16). Satan and his evil spirits are in a limited manner permitted to lie to and tempt people. The result is that every free moral agent is tested.

The sad truth of the matter is that every free moral agent has rebelled, and has "exchanged the truth of God for a lie" (Rom. 1:25). We can thank God, however, that He has provided a ransom for our sins and a way to be born into His family. Jesus' sacrificial death is the only and all-sufficient answer to our problem.

Satan's Deception, Now and Later

So we understand at least one reason why the devil and his rebel army are permitted to work on this planet: for the purpose of deceiving those who love darkness.

This truth is further validated when we consider that, according to the book of Revelation, Satan will one day be bound by an angel and incarcerated for a thousand years. The reason for his incarceration? "That he should not deceive the nations any longer" (Rev. 20:3). During that millennium, Jesus will personally rule the world from Jerusalem.

But after those thousand years, Satan will be released for a short period of time. The result? He "will come out to deceive the nations which are in the four corners of the earth" (Rev. 20:8).

Now then, if God didn't want Satan to deceive people at that time, then why would He release him? Especially in light of the fact that God originally incarcerated him "that he should not deceive the nations any longer"?

God, of course, would prefer that Satan never deceive anyone. But He knows that the only people whom Satan can deceive are those who don't believe what He Himself has said. Satan can only deceive those who reject the truth, and that is why God permits him to operate now, and why He will permit Satan to operate then. As Satan deceives people, the condition of people's hearts is made apparent, and then God can sort the "wheat from the tares" (see Matt. 13:24-30).

This is exactly what will happen at the end of the millennium when Satan is released. He will deceive all those who love darkness, and they will then gather their armies around Jerusalem in an attempt to overthrow Christ's rule. God will know exactly who loves Him and who hates Him, and thus He will immediately send "fire from heaven" that will "devour them" (Rev. 20:10). Satan will serve God's purposes then just as he does now. For this reason among others, it is foolish to think that we can "pull down territorial spirits." God allows them to operate for His own reasons.

Biblical Evangelism

The plain fact is that neither Jesus nor any of the New Testament apostles practiced the kind of spiritual warfare that some are claiming is the missing key to effective evangelism today. We never find Jesus, Peter, John, Stephen, Philip, or Paul "pulling down strongholds" or "binding the strong men" over the cities in which they preached. Rather, we find that they followed the Holy Spirit in regard to where He wanted them to preach; we find them proclaiming the simple gospel calling people to repentance and faith in Christ; and we find them enjoying marvelous results. And in those cases where they preached to unreceptive people who rejected the gospel, we don't find them "doing spiritual warfare so that Satan wouldn't be able to continue blinding their minds." Rather, we find them "shaking the dust off their feet" as Jesus commanded, and going to the next city (Matt. 10:14; Acts 13:5).

It is amazing that anyone could claim that "pulling down strongholds" and "binding the strong men" is a prerequisite to successful evangelism when there are so many thousands of examples of great revivals in church history where such "spiritual warfare" was never practiced.

"But our techniques work!" someone will say. "Since we started doing this kind of spiritual warfare, more people have been getting saved than ever before."

If that is true, I'll tell you why. It is because there has

been more scriptural prayer and evangelism done at the same time as your "spiritual warfare." Prayer and evangelism will bring a spiritual harvest, even if unscriptural things like "pulling down strongholds" over cities is done in conjunction.

What would you say if an evangelist told you, "Tonight, before I preached at the revival service, I privately did forty-one jumping jacks. And when I preached, sixteen people were saved! I've finally found the secret to effective evangelism! From now on, I'm going to make sure I do forty-one jumping jacks before I preach!"?

Surely you would say to that evangelist, "Your jumping jacks had nothing to do with those sixteen people being saved. The key to your success is that you preached the gospel, and there were sixteen people listening who were receptive."

God honors His Word. If God gives a promise, and someone meets the conditions to that particular promise, God will keep His promise, even if that person is doing other things that are unscriptural.

God Always Keeps His Promises

For example, I recently attended one of the most exploitive evangelistic crusades I have ever attended in my twenty years of being a Christian. It seemed that the evangelist used every trick in the book to get money, from "God told me there are 100 people here who are each supposed to give a thousand dollars," to "There is a special anointing right now for giving, and if you give generously right now, your act of faith will produce an extra-special return, and even some of your loved ones will be saved." The evangelist would blow on his crusade team to make them fall over "by the power of the Holy Spirit," and to me, it was about as convincing as studio wrestling on television. There was an incredible amount of showmanship, fakery, and hype, and I can't remember once hearing about Jesus dying on the cross for our sins.

At the end of the service, the evangelist claimed to have

the "word of knowledge" in operation. He then began calling out, supposedly by supernatural knowledge, general sicknesses and ailments that were afflicting people present in the large auditorium. (It's one thing when an evangelist points to a person in a crowd whom he doesn't know and says, "The Lord shows me you have a tumor in your kidney, and another thing when he points to a crowd of ten thousand and says, "The Lord shows me there are people here today who have back trouble"! That is not so convincingly supernatural.) He then encouraged them to receive their healings and come forward and testify of what God had done for them.

Amazingly enough, some people were genuinely healed! Why? Was it because the evangelist was so anointed by the Holy Spirit? No, it was because Jesus said, "All things for which you pray and ask, believe that you have received them, and they shall be granted you" (Mark 11:24). Sick people present in that crusade did what Jesus said to do, and Jesus did what He promised He would do. They believed and He healed them. Those who were healed didn't need to come to the crusade to wait for the "man of God" to call out their sickness; they could have received their healing at home by just taking God at His Word. But in spite of all that dishonored the Holy Spirit at that particular crusade, God still kept his Word for people who met His conditions.

It is the same way with the present spiritual warfare practices. If you start passing out tracts and "binding the strong man" over your city, a certain percentage of people will be saved. And, if you just start passing out tracts without binding the strong man, the same percentage of people will be saved.

How to Pray Scripturally For a Spiritual Harvest

How should we pray for unsaved people? First, we should understand that there is no instruction in the New Testament which tells us to pray that God will save people, nor is there any record of any early Christians praying that way. The reason is because, from God's standpoint, He has done everything He needs to do in order for everyone in the world to be saved. He so much desires for them to be saved that He gave His Son to die on the cross.

But why isn't everyone saved yet? Because not everyone has believed the gospel. And why have they not believed? There are only two reasons: (1) Either they have never yet heard the gospel, or (2) they've heard the gospel and rejected it.

That is why the scriptural way to pray for the unsaved is to pray that they will have opportunities to hear the gospel. For example, Jesus told us "The harvest is plentiful, but the laborers are few; therefore *beseech the Lord of the harvest to send out laborers into His harvest*" (Luke 10:2; italics mine). In order for people to hear the gospel and be saved, someone has to tell them the gospel. That is why we should pray for God to send people to them.

When the early church prayed regarding a spiritual harvest, they prayed, "Grant that Thy bond-servants may *speak Thy word with all confidence*, while Thou dost extend Thy hand to heal, and signs and wonders take place through the name of Thy holy servant Jesus" (Acts 4:29-30; italics mine).

They were asking either for (1) opportunities to proclaim the gospel boldly or (2) boldness to proclaim the gospel during the opportunities they knew they would have. They also expected God to confirm the gospel with healings, signs and wonders. Those are scriptural prayers, and notice the objective was to give people the opportunity to hear the gospel. God answered their prayer: "And when they had prayed, the place where they had gathered together was shaken, and they were all filled with the Holy Spirit, and began to speak the word of God with boldness" (Acts 4:31).

How did Paul think Christians should pray in regard to producing a spiritual harvest? Did he instruct them to ask God to save more people? No, let's read what he said:

Finally, brethren, *pray for us that the word of the Lord*

may spread rapidly and be glorified, just as it did also with you... (2 Thes. 3:1; italics mine).

Pray on my behalf, *that utterance may be given to me* in the opening of my mouth, *to make known with boldness the mystery of the gospel*, for which I am an ambassador in chains; *that in proclaiming it I may speak boldly*, as I ought to speak (Eph. 6:19-20; italics mine).

Whether or not people are saved now depends more upon them than it does upon God, and so our prayers should be for people to hear the gospel and for God to help us proclaim it. God will answer our prayers, but that still doesn't guarantee that anyone will be saved, because God gives people the right to make their own choices. Their salvation depends upon their response to the gospel.

Can We Not "Claim" People's Salvation?

In regard to this same subject of praying for the unsaved, is it not true that we can, by faith, claim certain people's salvation? Some Christians seem to think so, but there is no indication in the Bible that this is true. In fact, if it were true, then the entire biblical principle of free moral agency is negated.

How often I have heard people quote from Acts 16:31, claiming Paul's words there as a promise that all their relatives will be saved: "Believe in the Lord Jesus, and you shall be saved, you and your household."

But it is important that we read this sentence of Scripture contextually. Was Paul saying that if we believe, all of our household will be saved? No he was not. Paul was responding to a Philippian jailer who asked what he must do to be saved (Acts 16:30). It is quite obvious that Paul meant that if the jailer believed, he would be saved, and if his household believed, they would also be saved. That is why we read in the very next verse that Paul "spoke the word of the Lord to him *together with all who were in his house*" (Acts 16:32; italics mine). Paul spoke the gospel to everyone in the jailer's household because they each needed to believe individually in order to be saved. Jesus said, "God so loved the world, that He gave His only begotten Son, that whoever believes in Him should not perish... (John 3:16). He did not say, "Whoever's relative believes, he will not perish." Everyone must believe for himself.

As we continue reading the narrative in Acts 16, we find that all of the jailer's household did believe, and so Paul immediately baptized all of them in water:

> And he [the jailer] took them that very hour of the night and washed their wounds, and immediately he was baptized, he *and all his household.* And he brought them into his house and set food before them, and rejoiced greatly, having believed in God *with his whole household* (Acts 16:33-34; italics mine).

If we could simply claim, by faith, that our relatives would be saved, guaranteeing their salvation, why then did Paul write to the Corinthian Christians who had unsaved spouses, telling them, "For how do you know, O wife, whether you will save your husband? Or how do you know, O husband, whether you will save your wife?" (1 Cor. 7:16). The answer is that they don't know, which indicates that they can't simply "claim" the salvation of their spouses.

If we can claim the salvation of our household, why did Jesus say that because of His coming, "a man's enemies will be the members of his household" (Matt. 10:36)? And why did He say,

> "Do you suppose that I came to grant peace on earth? I tell you, no, but rather division; for from now on five members in one household will be divided, three against two, and two against three. They will be divided, father against son, and son against father; mother against daughter, and daughter against mother; mother-in-law against daughter-in-law, and daughter-in-law against mother-in-law" (Luke 12:51-53)?

Even though it is obvious from examining Scripture that we can't claim, "by faith," the salvation of our relatives (or anyone else), we can and should pray that God will send people across their paths to share gospel with them. And we should pray that God will give *us* opportunities and help *us* to share His truth with those who don't know Him.

Myth #6: "Spiritual warfare against territorial spirits opens the door for effective evangelism."

The truth is that there are no scriptures which instruct us to engage in battles with territorial spirits, nor are there any examples of any Christians doing so. God permits Satan and his hierarchy of evil spirits to rule the world of darkness in order to fulfill His divine purposes, and no amount of screaming at them by us will remove them. To try to "do spiritual warfare" against territorial spirits is a waste of time, and the idea that it will make any difference in evangelistic endeavors is unscriptural.

MYTH #7

Five Minor Myths

Myth #7A: "When a Christian sins, he opens the door for a demon to come and live in him."

It is true that when a Christian sins, it may be because he has yielded to temptation from an evil spirit. Yielding to the suggestion of an evil spirit, however, does not mean that the evil spirit himself is thus able to come inside the believer. If that were the case, every one of us would be so demon-possessed that we would all need to be locked away in padded cells, because as James wrote, "we all stumble in many ways" (Jas. 3:2).

When we sin as Christians, we break our *fellowship* with God, because we have disobeyed Him (see 1 Jn. 1:5-6). We feel guilty. We have not, however, broken our *relationship* with Him, as we are still His children.

If we confess our sins, "He is faithful and righteous to forgive us our sins and cleanse us from all unrighteousness" (1 Jn. 1:9). Then our fellowship with Him is restored. Notice

John did not say that we needed to be cleansed from any indwelling demons when we are guilty of sin.

Every Christian is faced with daily temptations from the world, the flesh, and the devil. Paul wrote that we do indeed have a struggle against various evil spirits (Eph 6:12). Therefore, to some degree, every believer is harassed by demon spirits. That is normal, and it is our responsibility to resist the devil and demons by faith in God's Word (1 Pet. 5:8-9). When we believe and act upon what God has said, that is resisting the devil.

For example, if Satan brings thoughts of depression, we should think on a scripture that counteracts depression, and obey God's Word to "rejoice always" (1 Thes. 5:16) and "give thanks in everything" (1 Thes. 5:18). It is our responsibility to act upon God's Word and replace Satan's thoughts with God's thoughts.

We must recognize that as free moral agents, we can think whatever we want to think about. If a believer continually *chooses* to listen and yield to the suggestions of evil spirits, he can certainly open his mind to being *oppressed*, which is simply a state of being more receptive to, and more dominated by, wrong thoughts. If he chooses to yield even more he could become *obsessed* with a certain kind of wrong thinking, which is very rare for a Christian, but can occur. Yet even then, if the obsessed Christian desires to be free, all he needs to do is determine to think about and yield to God's Words and resist the devil.

But could he ever become *possessed*? Only if he willfully decided, from his heart, without being pressured, to reject Christ and turn His back upon Him completely. Then, of course, he would no longer be a Christian[1] and thus potentially could become possessed—if he yielded himself all the more to the evil spirit that was oppressing him. But that is a far cry from the idea of opening the door for an evil spirit to inhabit you through committing one sin.

---

[1] Those who hold to the position of "once saved, always saved" will no doubt disagree. I would encourage them to read Rom. 11:22; 1 Cor. 15:1-2; Phil. 3:18-19; Col. 1:21-23 and Heb. 3:12-14, paying special attention to the word "if" whenever it is found.

It is a fact that there is not a single example in the New Testament of any Christian being possessed by a demon. Nor is there any warning addressed to Christians about the dangerous possibility of their being inhabited by demons. Nor is there any instruction regarding how to cast out demons from fellow-Christians.

The truth is that as Christians, we don't need demons cast out of us—what we need is to have our minds renewed upon the Word of God. That is scriptural. Paul wrote:

> And do not be conformed to this world, but be transformed by the renewing of your mind, that you may prove what the will of God is, that which is good and acceptable and perfect (Rom. 12:2).

Once our minds have been cleansed of old thinking patterns and have been renewed with the truth of God's Word, then we can gain victory over sinful habits and live in a consistent Christ-like manner. The truth is what sets us free (John 8:32). We are transformed as we renew our minds, not as we have all the demons exorcised!

Myth 7B: "Through studying the history of a city, we can determine which evil spirits are dominating it, and thus be more effective in spiritual warfare and ultimately in evangelization."

This myth is based upon several ideas that cannot be supported by Scripture. One such idea is that territorial spirits stick around for a long time. That is, the ones that lived over a region hundreds of years ago are supposedly the ones still there. Thus, if we find that a city was founded by greedy people, we can then conclude that there are spirits of greed that dominate the city today. If the city was once an old Indian village, we can conclude the spirits of shamanism and witchcraft dominate the city today. And on and on it goes.

But is it true that the same evil principalities and powers that lived over a geographical area hundreds of years ago are still there today? Perhaps, but not necessarily.

You no doubt remember the story we have considered previously from the tenth chapter of the book of Daniel. The unnamed angel who was assisted by Michael to fight "the prince of Persia" said to Daniel, "I shall now return to fight against the prince of Persia; so I am going forth, and behold, *the prince of Greece is about to come*" (Dan. 10:20). History tells us that the Persian empire fell to the Greeks through the conquests of Alexander the Great. Yet this unnamed angel was aware of imminent corresponding changes in the spiritual realm—the "prince of Greece" was coming.

When the prince of Greece did come, did he rule in the spiritual realm over the Greek empire just as the prince of Persia ruled in the spiritual realm over the Persian empire? It would seem to be a reasonable conclusion, and if so, then some high-ranking evil spirits changed geographical locations, as the Greek empire included practically all the territory of the Persian empire. When there are political changes on earth, there is a possibility that there are changes in the kingdom of darkness. In our nation, every election could potentially mark a change of powers in the spiritual realm. That fact is, however, that we just don't know unless the Lord would reveal it to us.

Regardless, it makes little difference what particular evil spirits are ruling over any given geographical area, as there is nothing we can do about it through "spiritual warfare," as proven in earlier chapters.

Over-Categorizing Evil Spirits

Moreover, it is an assumption on our part to think that there are ruling spirits that specialize in specific sins. The whole concept of there being "spirits of greed," "spirits of lust," "religious spirits," "spirits of strife," and so on, cannot be supported by Scripture, much less the idea that those different kinds of spirits exist in the higher ranks of evil spirits who rule the kingdom of darkness.

Amazing as it is to those who have never studied the four gospels closely, there are only three specific kinds of demons which Jesus cast out: Once a "dumb demon" is mentioned (Lk. 11:14), once we read of a "deaf and dumb spirit" (Mk. 9:25), and more than once we find reference to "unclean spirits," which seem to include all demons which Jesus exorcised, including even the "deaf and dumb" one (Mark 9:25).

And is it not possible that the "deaf and dumb spirit" was able to do something other than make someone deaf and dumb? There is no doubt it could, because it caused the boy of Mark 9 to have terrible seizures as well. There-fore "deaf and dumb" may not be a reference to the specific *type* of spirit it was but rather a simple reference as to *how it was harming* a certain individual. Many of us have become "category-crazy" when it comes to demons, but the Bible places no great emphasis on it.

In the entire Old Testament, the only specific spirits that are named that could *perhaps* be considered specific evil spirits are a "deceiving spirit" (1 Kings 22:22-23), a "spirit of distortion" (Is. 19:14), and a "spirit of harlotry" (Hos. 4:12; 5:4). In regard to the first and the second, certainly all evil spirits could be referred to as "deceiving spirits" and "spirits of distortion." In regard to the third, the phrase "spirit of harlotry" is not necessarily a refer-ence to a specific evil spirit, but simply a prevailing atti-tude.[2]

In the whole book of Acts, the only time a specific evil spirit is mentioned is in Acts 16:16, where we read about a young girl who had a "spirit of divination." And in all the epistles, the only kind of specific evil spirits that are mentioned are "deceitful spirits" (1 Tim. 4:1) which, again, could be a description of any evil spirit.

In light of the few references to specific kinds of demons in the Bible, it is amazing to read through some of the modern lists which contain hundreds of various kinds of demons that might inhabit people or control cities.

We should not assume there is any categorization, by

---

[2] The "spirit of jealousy" spoken of in Numbers 5:14-30 and the "spirit of haughtiness" of Proverbs 16:18 are good examples of the word *spirit* being used to convey a certain kind of predominant attitude, rather than an actual demon.

specific sin, of any higher ranks of evil spirits. It is an assumption to say, "Because there is so much gambling in that city, there must be gambling spirits over it."

Smoking Spirits?

Think how foolish someone would appear who said, "There must be many smoking spirits over that city, because so many people in that city smoke." What were those "smoking spirits" doing before those cities existed? Where were they then? What were they doing before tobacco was ever used for smoking? Is the reason fewer people are now smoking is because some of those old "smoking demons" are dying off or moving to new territories?

Do you see how foolish it is when we say such things as, "That city is controlled by spirits of lust, which is why there are so many topless bars there"? The truth is that wherever people are not serving Christ, there is the kingdom of darkness, and there are evil spirits who entice the subjects of that kingdom to sin and continue in their rebellion against God. Those spirits will tempt people in every area of sin, and in some places, people yield more to one sin than other sins. Their only hope is the gospel which we are called to proclaim.

Even if there were specific kinds of evil spirits who specialized in certain sins and who ruled certain geographical areas, it wouldn't help us to know about it, because there is nothing we can do to remove them. Our responsibility is to pray (in a scriptural manner) for the people there who are deceived and to preach the gospel to them.

The only good it would do to find out about the most predominate sins in a certain city would be so that we can preach more convicting messages to the unsaved living there—by specifically naming the sins that hold them guilty before God. But there is no need to research a city's history to determine that. One only needs to visit for a short while and keep his eyes and ears open. The predominant sins will soon become evident.

Finally, there is no example in the New Testament of anyone doing "spiritual mapping" as a means of preparing for spiritual warfare or evangelization. Nor are there any instructions in the epistles to do so. In the New Testament, the apostles followed the Holy Spirit in regard to where they should preach, faithfully proclaimed the simple gospel of Christ's substitutionary death and resurrection, and relied upon the Lord to confirm the word with signs following. Their method worked quite well.

Myth 7C: "We can be more effective in spiritual warfare for unsaved people if we pray 'on location.' Therefore, it is worthwhile to travel to foreign countries to do spiritual combat there."

If one wrongly assumes that he can do something to weaken the effectiveness of territorial spirits by shouting at them, then he might be fooled into thinking that the closer he got to them, the more effective he might be. For this reason, some Christians actually fly over population centers in helicopters in order to "pull down the strongholds," and some go to the tops of skyscrapers to scream at the "strong man" over their city.

All of this is a waste of time, as there is nothing anyone can to do to weaken any evil spirit's influence over a city other than challenge *people* to believe the truth of the gospel. Even if some people respond to the gospel and are saved, it doesn't weaken any demons. Those demons just have fewer people to deceive, but they are just as active as ever.

In regard to actually *praying to God* on behalf of unsaved people, there is no need to travel to the resident country in which they live to pray for them, because God hears our prayers no matter where we are.

Some may say they need to pray in foreign countries because it enables them to see first-hand the bondages and needs of unsaved people living there, and thus they can pray more specifically for them. However, all unsaved people need one thing more than anything else, and that is to hear the gospel. We can pray for that right where we are. That is why Jesus instructed us to pray that the Lord of the harvest would send laborers (Matt. 9:37-38), and why He commanded us to go into all the world and preach the gospel (Matt. 28:19).

There is no example in the New Testament of anyone journeying to a foreign city for the sole of purpose of praying for the inhabitants of that city. There are many examples, of course, of people journeying to distant cities in order to preach the gospel. This makes sense, as Jesus commanded us to go and preach, not go and pray. As it has been said by one, "You can pray for unsaved people until hell freezes over, but unless those people hear the gospel, the only difference your praying will make is that when those people go to hell, they will freeze instead of burn."

It is alarming to hear Christians exhuberantly report, "Since we started doing spiritual warfare for our city, the crime rate has dropped by 5%!" So what? Is anyone being saved? Are any disciples being made? Is our spiritual objective to lower crime rates or save people from hell?

No one can be saved unless he hears the gospel. How can we justify spending thousands of dollars on airfare to travel to foreign countries just to pray "on location" without ever sharing the gospel once we are there?

Myth 7D: "Some Christians need to be set free from generational or satanic curses."

The whole of idea of "generational curses" is derived from four passages of Scripture found in the Old Testament that all say essentially the same thing. They are Exodus 20:5; 34:7; Numbers 14:8 and Deuteronomy 5:9. Let's examine Numbers 14:18:

> The Lord is slow to anger and abundant in lovingkindness, forgiving iniquity and transgression; but He will by no means clear the guilty, *visiting the iniquity of the fathers on the children to the third and the fourth generations* (italics mine).

How are we to interpret this passage of Scripture? Does it mean that God will put a curse on or punish someone for the sins of his parents, grandparents, great grandparents, or great, great grandparents?

Absolutely not. Anyone who has any sense knows that would be unfair of God. He is, of course, completely righteous in His dealings with people. God Himself has stated that punishing someone for his parents' sins would be morally wrong:

> "Yet you say, 'Why should the son not bear the punishment for the father's iniquity?' When the son has practiced justice and righteousness, and has observed all My statutes and done them, he shall surely live. The person who sins will die. *The son will not bear the punishment for the father's iniquity, nor will the father bear the punishment for the son's iniquity*; the righteousness of the righteous will be upon himself, and the wickedness of the wicked will be upon himself" (Ezek. 18:19-20; italics mine).

Moreover, under the Law of Moses, God commanded that neither father or son should bear the punishment for the sins of the other:

> Fathers shall not be put to death for their sons, nor shall sons be put to death for their fathers; everyone shall be put to death for his own sin (Deut. 24:16).

There is no possibility that our God of love and righteousness might curse or punish someone for his ancestor's sins.[3] So then what does Scripture mean when it says that God will "by no means clear the guilty, visiting the iniquity of the fathers on the children to the third and the fourth generations"?

It can only mean that God holds people responsible for

---

[3] This is not to say that children don't suffer because of their parents' sins, because they often do. When they do, however, it is not an indication that God is punishing those children for their parents' sins, but an indication that people are so evil that they practice certain sins which they know will cause their own children to suffer.

the sinful example they set in front of their offspring, and He thus holds them partly responsible for the sins their offspring commit, since those offspring learned their sinful practice from their parents. God holds people partly responsible, because of their wrong example, for the sins of their great grandchildren! That is how holy God is. And no one can say that in doing so He is unfair.

Notice that the passage under consideration states that God will visit "the iniquity of the fathers on the children." It is the iniquity of fathers *on* their children that is being *visited.*

Thus, the whole idea of "generational curses" is a superstition.

Satanic Curses?

But what about "satanic curses"?

First, there is nothing in the entire Bible that indicates Satan is able to "put a curse" on anyone, nor are there any examples of his doing so. Certainly we find Satan afflicting people in the Bible, but never do we find him "putting a curse" on a family which then results in continual bad luck upon them and their successive generations.

Every Christian is harassed by Satan and evil spirits (to a limited extent) all of his life, but this does not mean that any of us need someone to "break a satanic curse" over us that has been passed down to us from our parents. What we need to do is stand on God's Word and resist the devil by faith, as we are told to do in the Scriptures (1 Pet. 5:8-9).

In the Bible, God is the one who has the power to bless and curse (see Gen. 3:17; 4:11; 5:29; 8:21; 12:3; Num. 23:8; Deut. 11:26; 28:20; 29:27; 30:7; 2 Chron. 34:24; Ps. 37:22; Prov. 3:33; 22:14; Lam. 3:65; Mal. 2:2; 4:6). Others may curse us with their mouths, but their curses are powerless to harm us:

> Like a sparrow in its flitting, like a swallow in its flying, so a curse without cause does not alight (Prov. 26:2).

Balaam had it right when, after being hired by Balak to

curse the children of Israel, he said, "How shall I curse, whom God has not cursed? And how can I denounce, whom the Lord has not denounced?" (Num. 23:8).

Some Christians have gone overboard on the idea of people placing curses on other people based upon Jesus' words in Mark 11:23: "Truly I say to you, whoever says to this mountain, 'Be taken up and cast into the sea,' and does not doubt in his heart, but believes that what he says is going to happen, it shall be granted him."

Notice, however, that there is no power in just speaking words, but rather, in speaking words that are believed from the heart. There is no way a person could have faith that his curse against someone could actually bring harm to that person, because faith is a confident assurance (Heb. 11:1), and faith only comes from hearing God's Word (Rom. 10:17). A person might *hope* his curse against someone will bring misfortune, but he could never *believe* it, because God has given no promise about cursing people which could supply him with faith.

The only exception to this would be if God gave someone "the gift of faith" along with a "gift of prophecy" (two of the nine gifts of the Spirit), that would be spoken in the form of a blessing or curse, as we see He occasionally did in the lives of some Old Testament characters (see Gen. 27:27-29, 38-41; 49:1-27; Josh. 6:26 with 1 Kin. 16:34; Judg. 9:7-20, 57; 2 Kin. 2:23-24). Even in those cases, the blessings or curses originated from *God*, not man. Thus, the whole idea of someone being able to "place a curse" on another person is just a superstition. This is why Jesus did not instruct us to "break any curses that have been spoken against us" but rather to simply "bless those who curse us." We do not need to be afraid of any person's curses!

Occult Curses?

Is it possible to have some satanic curse upon us because of past involvement in the occult?

We must not forget that when we are saved, we are delivered from Satan's power and the kingdom of darkness

(Acts 26:18; Col. 1:13). Satan no longer has any hold on us unless we give it to him. Although the Bible indicates that the Ephesian Christians were heavily involved in practicing magic before their conversion (Acts 19:18-19), there is no record of Paul breaking any "Satanic curses" or binding Satan's power over them after they were saved. The reason is because they were automatically set free from Satan's dominion the moment they first believed in Jesus.

Additionally, when Paul wrote to the Ephesian Christians, he gave no instructions regarding setting anyone free from generational or satanic curses. All he told them was to "not give the devil an opportunity" (Eph. 4:27), and to "put on the full armor of God" that they might "be able to stand firm against the schemes of the devil" (Eph. 6:11). Those are every Christian's responsibilities.

But why, in some cases, have Christians apparently been helped when someone broke a "generational" or "satanic curse" over them? Simply because the individual who needed help had faith that the devil would flee once the "curse" was broken. Faith is what puts the devil on the run, and every Christian can and should have faith that when he resists the devil, the devil will flee. There is no need to call in a "deliverance specialist" in order to send Satan running.

Finally, the Bible tells us that Christ "became a *curse* for us," and in so doing, "redeemed us from the *curse* of the Law" (Gal 3:13; italics mine). All of us were formerly under God's curse because we had sinned, but since Jesus bore our punishment, we have been released from that curse. Praise God! No longer cursed, we can rejoice that we have now been *blessed* "with every spiritual blessing in the heavenly places in Christ" (Eph. 1:3).

Myth 7E: "We can break demonic bondages through fasting."

Some Christians seem to regard fasting as one of the most preeminent aspects of Christian life and responsibility. This is quite amazing in light of the fact that in all the epistles of the New Testament, there is not one instruction given to Christians regarding fasting. Nowhere in the epistles are Christians even encouraged to fast. In fact, the epistles have nothing at all to say about fasting, other than Paul's mention of a few times when he had to go hungry, examples of involuntary fasting.

In the book of Acts, there are only two examples of voluntary fasting:

> And while they were ministering to the Lord and *fasting*, the Holy Spirit said, "Set apart for Me Barnabas and Saul for the work to which I have called them." Then, when they had *fasted* and prayed and laid their hands on them, they sent them away (Acts 13:2-3; italics mine).

> And when they had appointed elders for them in every church, having prayed with *fasting*, they commended them to the Lord in whom they had believed (Acts 14:23; italics mine)

We learn that the primary benefit of fasting under the new covenant is to give us more time to concentrate on prayer. This is especially important when we are seeking God for specific direction, as we wait for His guidance to become clear within our own spirits.

In ancient times, the preparation and eating of meals was much more time consuming than it is today, and by fasting, people were afforded much more time to pray. That is the primary reason to abstain from eating.

As every Christian knows, probably the most difficult thing about spending extended time in prayer is finding the time to do it. Sometimes the only way to find a few hours to pray is to eliminate something else. That is probably why Jesus once prayed all night (notice it was before He chose His apostles), and why He often rose early in the morning to pray. That is why Paul wrote to married Christians and told them not to deprive their spouses of sexual relations, "except by agreement for a time *that you may devote yourselves to prayer*" (1 Cor. 7:5; italics mine).

In order to spend an extended time of prayer, we may have to abstain from some of the legitimate pleasures of life, such as sleep, sex, or food.

Fast or Hunger Strike?

Fasting does not change God. We shouldn't think that because we are afflicting ourselves by fasting, God will more readily listen to our prayers. That would be more like a hunger strike! We don't need to gain God's attention by fasting—we already have His attention when we pray according to His will (see 1 John 5:14).

Fasting does not give us more spiritual power or give us authority over demons. As members of Christ's body, we already are "seated in heavenly places, far above all rule and authority and power and dominion, and every name that is named" (Eph. 1:21). We already have the authority to cast out demons according to Jesus' promise in Mark 16:17: "And these signs will accompany those who have believed: in My name they will cast out demons..."

But what about Jesus' statement concerning a demon He once exorcised: "But this kind does not go out except by prayer and fasting" (Matt. 17:21)?

First, my Bible indicates that many of the original manuscripts of Matthew's gospel do not contain this particular verse, which means it is possible that Jesus never said, "This kind does not go out except by prayer and fasting."

In Mark's account of the same incident, Jesus is recorded as saying, "This kind cannot come out by anything but prayer" (Mark 9:29), and it is noted in the margin that many manuscripts add "and fasting" to the end of the verse.

So did Jesus say that fasting is a necessary ingredient in exercising a particular kind of demon? The answer is that we don't know. Nevertheless, if Jesus did actually make the statement regarding fasting, that is the only time He or any of the New Testament writers associated fasting with deliverance from a demon.

Perhaps it would be helpful to ask ourselves how fasting could be an aid in exorcising demons. Certainly fasting could not increase anyone's authority over demons; if God has given one authority to cast out demons, he has it. The only thing that fasting could do would be provide one with more time to meditate on God's promise of his authority, thus increasing his faith in what God has said.

In the case under consideration, the disciples had previously been given authority to cast out unclean spirits (see Matt. 10:1), but they failed to cast out a demon from a young boy. When Jesus heard of their failure, He immediately lamented their unbelief (Matt. 17:17), and when they asked Him why they failed, He responded, "Because of the littleness of your faith" (Matt. 17:20). It is a few verses later that we find Jesus' questionable statement concerning fasting.

Thus we can conclude the reason for their failure as being one of two possibilities: Either they didn't have faith in their God-given authority *plus* they didn't pray and fast beforehand, or they didn't have faith in their God-given authority, and time spent in fasting and prayer could have helped them build their faith. I would prefer to accept the second scenario, as it makes more sense, while the first seems to make Jesus contradict Himself. Keep in mind that both possibilities are predicated upon the assumption that Jesus actually made the statement about fasting.

Regardless of the correct interpretation, we must not forget that the overwhelming majority of references to spiritual warfare and deliverance from demons make no mention of fasting. There is no mention at all of fasting in connection with our *personal warfare* against Satan and evil spirits, and to say that we must fast to gain personal victory over the devil is entirely unscriptural.

The Fast That God Chooses

One other passage of Scripture that is often misconstrued to prove that fasting can break demonic bondages is Isaiah 58:6:

> Is this not the fast which I choose, to loosen the bonds of wickedness, to undo the bands of the yoke,

and to let the oppressed go free, and break every yoke? (Is. 58:6).

Does this verse of Scripture teach that we can break demonic bondages over people by fasting? It can only when it is taken out of context and then assumptions are added to it. But when read in context and no assumptions are added, it clearly does not.

Let's beat Satan at one of his games (taking scriptures out of context), and read most of the fifty-eighth chapter of Isaiah to learn what God was actually saying:

> "Cry loudly, do not hold back; raise your voice like a trumpet, and declare to My people their transgression, and to the house of Jacob their sins" (Is. 58:1)

Here God is speaking to Isaiah, commissioning him to declare to Israel their sins. In the very next verse, God begins to enumerate those sins:

> "Yet they seek Me day by day, and delight to know My ways, as a nation that has done righteousness, and has not forsaken the ordinance of their God. They ask Me for just decisions, they delight in the nearness of God" (Is. 58:2).

Here is revealed Israel's hypocrisy. They claimed to be righteous, but their religion was just a facade. They were only going through the motions of devotion. They asked God,

> "'Why have we fasted and Thou dost not see? Why have we humbled ourselves and Thou dost not notice?'" (Is. 58:3a).

And God responded:

> Behold, on the day of your fast you find *your desire, and drive hard all your workers.* Behold, you fast for *contention and strife and to strike with a wicked fist.* You do not fast like you do today to make your voice heard on high. Is it a fast like this which I choose, a day for a man to humble himself? Is it for bowing one's head like a reed, and for spreading out sack-

cloth and ashes as a bed? *Will you call this a fast, even an acceptable day to the Lord?"* (Is. 58:3b-5; italics mine).

Apparently, they had been fasting to gain God's attention or favor, and wondered why their situation hadn't improved. God responded by reminding them of their selfish lifestyles, displayed even during the days of their fasting. Additionally, their reasons for fasting were purely selfish. God said it was completely unacceptable. Then He tells them about the kind of fast He is looking for—a fasting from selfishness:

> "Is this not the fast which I choose, to loosen the bonds of wickedness, to undo the bands of the yoke, and to let the oppressed go free, and break every yoke? Is it not to divide your bread with the hungry, and bring the homeless poor into the house; when you see the naked, to cover him; and not to hide yourself from your own flesh? (Is. 58:6-7).

Is God saying that if they fast, it will set people free from demonic bondage? Not at all. God wants them to abstain, not from food, but from being selfish. He wants them to love their neighbor as themselves. He wants them to break yokes,"let the oppressed go free," divide their bread with the hungry, bring the homeless poor into their houses, and cover the naked. The act of abstaining from food by itself will not result in any of those things. Those are things *people* must do.

This interpretation becomes even more clear as we continue reading. If the Israelites would begin to fast from their self-centered lifestyles, God promised,

> "Then your light will break out like the dawn, and your recovery will speedily spring forth; and your righteousness will go before you; the glory of the Lord will be your rear guard. Then you will call, and the Lord will answer; you will cry, and He will say, 'Here I am.' If *you remove the yoke from your midst, the pointing of the finger, and speaking wickedness, and if*

you give yourself to the hungry, and satisfy the desire of
the afflicted, then your light will rise in darkness, and
your gloom will become like midday" (Is. 58:8-10;
italics mine).

Verse 9 makes it very clear that God is not talking about
Himself removing some demonic yoke in response to their
fasting. Rather, He is telling them that _they_ are the ones
who should be removing, not demonic, but human yokes
from people, such as injustice and poverty. God was much
more interested in the Israelites abstaining from selfishness than He was in their abstaining from food. This is no
doubt true for us as well. The second greatest command-
ment is not, "Make sure you fast often," but "You shall love
your neighbor as yourself" (Mark 12:31).

The idea that we can break people free from Satan's
grasp by the act of fasting is erroneous. The primary way
to get people set free from Satan is to tell them the gospel.
If they respond with faith, they'll be set free. Then we can
teach them how to resist the devil by faith in God's Word.

EIGHT

Scriptural Spiritual Warfare

I had just delivered a sermon on how to resist the devil by faith in God's Word. Innocently, being a guest speaker, I had mentioned a popular teaching that many Christians had embraced concerning the demonic nature of owls and frogs. During that particular time in the late seventies, deliverance was a very "hot" topic; there was much extreme teaching, and it was thought by many that you could open your home to an invasion of demons if you had any pictures of owls or frogs hanging there!

The whole teaching was built upon a few verses in the Old Testament about owls being unclean animals and one verse in Revelation that describes some demons that resembled frogs. Still, many Christians in my audience that day were stunned when I told them I had several pictures of owls hanging in my house, and even possessed a ceramic frog, but I was not afraid of any demons gaining entrance to my home. I explained to them that *God* is the one who created owls and frogs, and that there was nothing in the Bible that even intimated that we could open our homes to demons if we had a ceramic frog by our fireplace. I told them that any Christian who was afraid of pictures of owls was a Christian who did not believe God's Word that "greater is He who is in you than he who is in the world" (1 Jn. 4:4).

As soon as my sermon was finished and the people were dismissed by the pastor, a woman in the congregation hurried to the front of the church and cornered me. "I heard your comments about owls and frogs," she said, "but you are entirely wrong. Let me tell you what happened to us!" (I immediately recognized that I was dealing with a person whose theology was built upon her experiences, rather than the Word of God.)

She told me her story. "Several months ago, my husband and I began to notice some very strange things were happening in our home. In the middle of the night, we would hear noises." (I thought to myself, *So what? Anyone who listens for noises in the night will hear them.*) She continued: "Sometimes, when I would be taking a shower, the temperature of the water would suddenly change!" *(That happens every time I'm taking a shower and someone flushes a toilet or turns the water on somewhere else in the house.)* "Sometimes, when I would open the refrigerator door, things inside would just fall out onto the floor for no reason." *(That happens all the time when my kids don't put things back properly into the refrigerator.)*

I was waiting for her to tell me that sometimes, when she washed her husband's socks in the washing machine, some of his socks mysteriously disappeared, but she didn't!

"So we called pastor so-and-so, whom God really uses in the area of deliverance, and he came over to investigate. He walked through our house anointing everything with oil and casting out Satan while looking for avenues which may have provided entrance for demonic activity in our home."

She then told me that when pastor so-and-so came to

her son's room, he sensed an evil presence there, and, upon opening the toy box, discovered the reason for all their troubles. There it was—gasp!—Kermit the frog! That stuffed toy had opened the door for demons to invade their home!

Ashes to Ashes...

But that is not the end of the story. They took poor Kermit out to their back yard to burn him. "It was bizarre," she said, "It was next to impossible to get that thing to burn." (Again I thought to myself, *All stuffed toys are made of inflammable material for safety reasons.*) "And when it did finally burn, it gave off this really strange odor!" (I was not surprised to learn that inflammable materials emit strange odors when burned!) And ever since the burning of Kermit, things had dramatically improved in their home.

When her story was over, I felt sorry for Kermit, but I felt even sorrier for her. As long as our Christian life is based upon experiences rather than on what God says, we are wide open for deception. I wondered how long it would be before she and her husband would have another imaginary battle with demons.

That woman is a representative of so many Christians who are more conscious of the devil and demons than of God. Some are always involved in a great battle with the devil, and they start each day, not in prayer and Bible study, but in binding demons in their bedrooms. Some of them hide in their homes on Halloween night, fearfully praying that God will protect them from all the wicked spirits that are out that evening. Some of them are afraid of being cursed through the prayers of Christians who dislike them. Some of them are joining other militant Christians on the tops of tall buildings in order to shout at the principalities and powers and pull down the "strong man" over their town. All of them are missing out on the blessing of knowing what the Bible really says about spiritual warfare. And whether they realize it or not, all of them are losing the very battle that they are trying to win, because they believe something other than what God has said. Satan has deceived them.

First and Foremost...

The first thing we should know about spiritual warfare is that it should not be the focus of our Christian life. We should be focused on Christ, to follow and obey Him, as we progressively grow to be more like Him. Only a small percentage of the New Testament writings address the subject of spiritual warfare, indicating to us that it should be a minor focus in the Christian life.

The second thing we should know about spiritual warfare is that the Bible tells us what we need to know. We don't need any special discernment (or a preacher who claims to have special discernment) into the "deep things of Satan." Biblical spiritual warfare is simple. Satan's schemes are clearly revealed in Scripture. Our responsibilities are straightforwardly outlined. Once you know and believe what God has said, you are a guaranteed winner in this spiritual struggle.

Back to the Beginning

Let's go back to the book of Genesis, where we are first introduced to the devil. In the Bible I use, Satan appears on page 2 in the form of a serpent. If there is any doubt that this serpent is the devil, Revelation 20:2 removes it: "And he laid hold of the dragon, *the serpent of old*, who is the devil and Satan..." (italics mine).

Genesis 3:1 tells us that "the serpent was more crafty than any beast of the field which the Lord God had made." When you think about how crafty some of God's creatures are as they compete to survive and stalk their prey, it makes you realize how cunning Satan must be. On the other hand, Satan is not all-knowing or all-wise as God is, and we should not assume that we are at a mental disadvantage in our struggle against him. Jesus instructed *us* to be as "shrewd as *serpents*" (Matt. 10:16; italics mine). Paul claimed that he was not ignorant of Satan's schemes (2 Cor. 2:11) and that we have the "mind of Christ" (1 Cor. 2:16).

Satan launched his first recorded fiery dart by questioning Eve concerning what God has said. Her response would reveal to him whether he had a chance at deceiving her into being disobedient. *Satan has no avenue to defeat anyone who believes and obeys what God has said, which is why his entire strategy revolves around ideas that contradict God's Word.*

Satan asked her, "Indeed, has God said, 'You shall not eat from any tree of the garden'?" (Gen. 3:1.) It almost sounds like an innocent question from an casual inquirer, but Satan knew exactly what his goal was.

Eve responded, "From the fruit of the trees of the garden we may eat; but from the fruit of the tree which in the middle of the garden, God has said, 'You shall not eat from it or touch it, lest you die'" (Gen. 3:2-3).

Eve almost had it right. Actually, God never forbid them to *touch* the tree of the knowledge of good and evil, but only forbid eating from it. Perhaps her husband, who may have passed God's original command on to her, thought it might insure her holiness if he added the part about touching the tree. If that is true, in doing so, Adam became the first of God's many spokespersons who add their own embellishments to His Word!

Eve did, however, know enough of the truth to recognize the lie of Satan's response: "You surely shall not die!" (Gen. 3:4).

That, of course, is a blatant contradiction of what God said, and it would be unlikely that Eve would buy it outright. So Satan then sugar-coated his lie with some truth, making it much easier to swallow, as he often does today. He continued: "For God knows that in the day you eat from it your eyes will be opened, and you will be like God, knowing good and evil" (Gen. 3:5).

Satan actually made three truthful statements directly after his lie. Once Adam and Eve ate the forbidden fruit, their eyes *were* opened (Gen. 3:7). Additionally, God Himself later said that the man *had* become like God and that he *had* come to know good and evil (Gen. 3:22). Satan often mixes truth with error in order to deceive people.

Notice also that Satan maligned God's character. God didn't want Adam and Eve to eat the forbidden fruit for their own well-being and happiness, but Satan made it sound as if God was withholding something from them that was wonderful. The majority of Satan's lies malign God's character, will, and motives.

Unfortunately, Earth's first couple rejected the truth to believe a lie, and they suffered the consequences. But notice all the elements of modern spiritual warfare in their story: Satan's only weapon was a lie couched in truth. The humans were faced with a choice to believe what God had said or what Satan had said. Believing the truth could have been their "shield of faith," but they never lifted it.

Adam and Eve lost God's best and were expelled from paradise, and the serpent was cursed to crawl on his belly and eat dust all the days of his life. We, of course, know that every snake today crawls on its belly, but is it possible that Satan must also? It is obvious that God's curse addressed to the serpent has more application than just to snakes (see Gen. 3:15). Perhaps we should envision Satan not as a powerful angelic figure standing proudly in the heavenly places, but as a groveling snake-like creature who squirms along with his face in the dirt.

Spiritual Warfare and the Second Adam

As we read the account of Jesus' encounter with Satan during His wilderness temptation, we quickly see that Satan had not changed his methods over thousands of years. His avenue of attack was to discredit what God had said, as he knew that his only way of defeating his enemy was to dissuade Him from believing or obeying the truth. *God's Word is again at the center of the battle.* Satan volleys a lie, and Jesus deflects it with truth. That is biblical spiritual warfare.

Jesus had been baptized by John a few weeks earlier, and God had spoken audibly at that event, saying, "This is My beloved Son, in whom I am well-pleased" (Matt. 3:17).

Not surprisingly then, Satan's first attack against Jesus involved what God had just declared about Him. Satan said to Jesus, *"If You are the Son of God*, command that these stones become bread"* (Matt. 4:3; italics mine).

Was Satan doubtful that Jesus was God's Son, thus desiring some convincing proof, or was he attempting to cause Jesus to doubt who He was? I'm not sure. I suspect, however, that the second scenario is a better possibility. It is difficult for me to believe that Satan wasn't already convinced that Jesus was the Son of God in light of the events that surrounded His birth.

Additionally, although there is much mystery concerning Christ's incarnation, we know that Jesus was not born with a fully-developed adult mind, and thus it was at some point in his childhood when He actually knew and could say He was God's Son. God the Father revealed it to Him, and so it was something He could have chosen to believe or not believe; this was just as true concerning what He heard spoken from heaven at His baptism. Therefore, perhaps the devil was attempting to cause Jesus to doubt who God said He (Jesus) was.

Regardless of whether this particular interpretation is true, that does not discount the fact that Satan will attempt to cause us to doubt what God has said about us. For example, we are told in the Bible that we are sons of God through faith in Christ (Gal. 3:26). Satan would prefer that we not believe that, because whether we do or not makes a big difference in how we will live our daily lives. The devil will, therefore, lie to us in that regard.

Another (and no doubt more traditional) interpretation of Jesus' first temptation is that Satan, capitalizing on Jesus' hunger, was tempting Him simply to disobey God's decree in Deuteronomy 8:3 that man shall not live on bread alone. In other words, if Satan had said, "Command these stones to become bread *and potatoes*," then it would not have been a sin for Jesus to do so.

This interpretation, rather than the first one I mentioned, is supported by the fact that Jesus did not respond to Satan by saying, "Oh yes, I am the Son of God! God said I was!" Rather, His response seems to indicate that the real temptation was not doubting He was the Son of God, but rather to disobey God's decree concerning living on bread alone.

I'm sure there is much more to Jesus' first temptation than any of us realize, and I would love to dig deeper in our investigation to bring out every possible point of consideration. It would, however, serve no good purpose as far as our subject is concerned and so I will conclude and proceed to the second temptation. It is important, however, that we understand that Jesus was faced with the same situation as Eve, Adam, and all the rest of us. He had to decide if He would listen to God or Satan. Jesus fought His spiritual battle with the "sword of the Spirit," the Word of God.

The Second Temptation

Matthew tells us:

> Then the devil took Him into the holy city; and he had Him stand on the pinnacle of the temple, and said to Him, "If You are the Son of God throw Yourself down; for it is written, 'He will give His angels charge concerning You'; and 'On their hands they will bear You up, lest You strike Your foot against a stone.'" Jesus said to him, "On the other hand, it is written, 'You shall not put the Lord your God to the test'" (Mark 4:5-7).

Here again the central issue is what God has said. This time, Satan even quoted God's Word from the ninety-first Psalm, but He twisted it in an attempt to make it mean something that God never intended.

Jesus responded by quoting a scripture that brought a balanced understanding of God's promises of protection found in Psalm 91. God will protect us, but not if we act foolishly, "putting Him to the test," as the note in the margin of my Bible indicates.

This is why it is so vital that we not wrench Bible verses out of context from the rest of Bible. Every scripture must be balanced with what the rest of Scripture says.

Twisting Scripture is one of Satan's most common tactics in spiritual warfare, and sadly, he has been very successful using that tactic against many Christians who are caught up in the modern spiritual warfare movement. A classic example of such twisting is the use of the biblical phrase "pulling down strongholds" to support the idea of pulling down evil spirits in the atmosphere. As I discussed in an earlier chapter, that particular phrase, when read in context, has absolutely no application to the pulling down of evil spirits in the atmosphere. Yet the devil would love for us to think it does, so we can waste our time screaming at the principalities and powers in the sky!

This second temptation also began with Satan saying, "If you are the Son of God..." There is again the possibility that Satan was attempting to cause Jesus to doubt who He was.

A more traditional interpretation of this second incident is that it was a temptation for Jesus to gain people's attention by using His power for something other than truly beneficial miracles, such as physical healing or raising someone from the dead, and so on.

The main point is that Jesus overcame Satan's temptation by knowing and acting upon God's Word. Hopefully, all of us, if faced with a similar temptation, would know enough of God's Word to recognize when Satan is twisting it.

The Third Temptation

The third temptation is perhaps the easiest to understand. Matthew writes:

> Again, the devil took Him to a very high mountain, and showed Him all the kingdoms of the world, and their glory; and he said to Him, "All these things will I give You, if You fall down and worship me." Then Jesus said to him, "Begone, Satan! For it is written,

'You shall worship the Lord your God, and serve Him only.'" (Matt. 4:8-10).

This was a temptation for power. If Jesus had worshipped Satan, and if Satan then kept his end of the bargain, Jesus would have gained the second-in-command position over the kingdom of darkness. He would have ruled over every unsaved human being and every evil spirit, having world-wide influence as only Satan had previously. We can only speculate in our nightmares what would have happened had Jesus yielded to that temptation.

Notice again that Jesus countered Satan's suggestion with the written Word of God. During each of the three temptations, Jesus overcame by saying, "It is written." We, too, must know God's Word and believe it if we want to avoid being deceived and fall into Satan's traps. That is what spiritual warfare is all about.

Satan's Strategy

Some Christians have the idea the devil and demons have the power to stop their cars from running, to send rain on their picnics, and to change the temperature of the water when they are taking a shower. But, for the most part, the only power that Satan and his demons have is to plant thoughts in people's hearts and minds (and even that is limited by God; see 1 Cor. 10:13). With that thought in mind, consider the following sampling of scriptures:

> But Peter said, "Ananias, why has *Satan filled your heart to lie to the Holy Spirit, and to keep back some of the price of the land?*" (Acts 5:3; italics mine).

> And during supper, *the devil having already put into the heart of Judas Iscariot, the son of Simon, to betray Him...* (John 13:2; italics mine).

> But the Spirit explicitly says that in later times some will fall away from the faith, *paying attention to deceitful spirits and doctrines of demons...* (1 Tim. 4:1; italics mine).

But I am afraid, lest *as the serpent deceived Eve by his craftiness, your minds should be led astray* from the simplicity and purity of devotion to Christ (2 Cor. 11:3; italics mine).

Stop depriving one another, except by agreement for a time that you may devote yourselves to prayer, and come together again *lest Satan tempt you* because of your lack of self-control (1 Cor. 7:5; italics mine).

For this reason, when I could endure it no longer, I also sent to find out about your faith, for fear that *the tempter might have tempted you, and our labor should be in vain* (1 Thes. 3:5; italics mine).

...in whose case t*he god of this world has blinded the minds of the unbelieving*, that they might not see the light of the gospel of the glory of Christ, who is the image of God (2 Cor. 4:4; italics mine).

And the great dragon was thrown down, the serpent of old who is called the devil and Satan, *who deceives the whole world*; he was thrown down to the earth, and his angels were thrown down with him (Rev. 12:9; italics mine).

"You are of your father the devil, and you want to do the desires of your father. He was a murderer from the beginning, and *does not stand in the truth, because there is no truth in him. Whenever he speaks a lie, he speaks from his own nature; for he is a liar, and the father of lies*" (John 8:44; italics mine).

The Battle Ground

These scriptures and others make it clear that the primary battle ground in biblical spiritual warfare is our hearts and minds. Satan attacks with thoughts—evil suggestions, wrong ideas, false philosophies, temptations, various lies and so on. Our means of defense is knowing, believing, and acting upon God's Word.

It is vitally important that you understand that every

thought you think does not necessarily originate from within yourself. Satan has many spokespersons who help him plant his thoughts in people's minds. He works to influence us through newspapers, books, television, magazines, radio, through friends and neighbors, and even through preachers. Even the apostle Peter was once unwittingly used as a spokesman for Satan, suggesting to Jesus that it was not God's will for Him to die (see Matt. 16:23).

But Satan and evil spirits also work directly on human minds, without any human intermediary, and all Christians will at times find themselves under direct assault. That is when the warfare begins.

I remember a dear Christian woman who once came to me to confess a problem. She said that whenever she prayed, she found that blasphemous thoughts and swear words would come to her mind. She was one of the sweetest, kindness, dearest, most dedicated women in my church, yet she had this problem with terrible thoughts.

I explained to her that those thoughts did not originate within her, but that she was being attacked by Satan, who was attempting to wreck her prayer life. She then told me she has stopped praying every day because she was so afraid she might think those thoughts again. Satan had succeeded.

So I told her to start praying again, and if those blasphemous thoughts came to her mind, she should counteract them with truth from God's Word. If a thought said to her, "Jesus was just a ———, she should say, "No, Jesus was and is the divine Son of God." If a thought came that was a swear word, she should replace that thought with a thought of praise for Jesus, and so on.

I also told her that by being afraid that she might think wrong thoughts, she was actually inviting them, as fear is somewhat of a reverse faith—a faith in the devil. By trying not to think about something, we have to think about it in order to try not to think about it!

For example, if I say to you, "Don't think about your right

hand," you will immediately think about your right hand as you attempt to obey me. The harder you try, the worse it gets. The only way not to think about your right hand is to consciously think about something else, for example, your shoes. Once you have your mind on your shoes, you are not thinking about your hand.

I encouraged that dear woman to "fear not," just as the Bible commands us. And whenever she recognized a thought that was contrary to God's Word, she should replace it with one that agreed with God's Word.

I'm happy to report that she followed my advice, and, although attacked a few more times during her prayer times, she gained complete victory over her problem. She triumphed in biblical spiritual warfare.

It has also been interesting for me to discover, upon taking surveys in a number of churches, that her problem was very common. Usually more than half of the Christians I survey indicate that at one time or another, they have had blasphemous thoughts while praying. Satan is not so original.

"Take Care What You Listen To"

We cannot stop Satan and evil spirits from attacking our minds, but we don't have to allow *their* thoughts to become *our* thoughts. That is, we don't have to dwell upon demonic ideas and suggestions, taking possession of them. As it has been said by someone, "You can't keep the birds from flying over your head, but you can keep them from making a nest in your hair."

Additionally, we should be careful not to subject our minds to ungodly influences whenever it is within our control. When we sit down in front of the television for an hour, or read the newspaper, we are putting out the welcome mat to be influenced with thoughts that may be satanic. Directly after He told the parable of the sower and the soils, Jesus warned, "Take care what you listen to" (Mark 4:24). Jesus knew the destructive effects of listening to lies, allowing Satan to plant his "seeds" in our hearts and minds. Those seeds may grow up into "thorns and thistles" which will ultimately choke the Word of God from our lives (see Mark 4:7, 18-19).

A Personal Example

One particular example of spiritual warfare in my own life is so personal I hesitate to share it, but I will because I think it will help some of my readers.

Some years ago, while I was engaged in conversation with a friend, I suddenly found myself thinking about kissing that person on the lips! Most alarming was the fact that the person I was speaking with was of the same sex! I was immediately repulsed, and I'm sure that my alarm was evident to my friend, although he didn't question me about it.

Then the thought came to me: *Face it, David, you are a homosexual.* I didn't know quite as much spiritually as I know now, but praise God I was able to recognize that thought as being from the devil.

Over the next few days, several more times, while I was engaged in conversation with male friends and acquaintances, I had those same perverted and troubling thoughts. Looking back, I think my great concern over it added to the problem, as I tried so hard not to think those thoughts again.

Eventually I realized what was happening, and the next time those thoughts came, I said in my mind, *No devil, I'm not a homosexual, I'm a normal human male who is also a child of God.* Then I would immediately replace that alarming, perverted thought with the thought of kissing my wife. I got victory quickly!

I have since wondered if that is how some men actually do become homosexuals. I do not believe they are born that way, but that at some point they begin to *believe* that they are different from other men. *Perhaps* because of ill feelings toward his mother, a young man finds himself, quite innocently, more attracted to males, and Satan capitalizes on those feelings and slowly convinces him he is a homosexual. *Perhaps* because a man never felt accepted by his father, he innocently seeks for acceptance from other males, and Satan uses those feelings to feed him lies about his sexual identity.

I'm not saying that these are the reasons all homosexuals are like they are, I'm only suggesting a few possibilities, knowing something about how Satan operates. I'm sure there are plenty of men who are homosexuals simply because they are in complete rebellion against God, and their sexual lives are just one of numerous indications of their depravity.

The hope for any homosexual is, of course, believing in Jesus and becoming one of His followers. Then he will be transformed and gain total victory as his mind is renewed upon God's Word (Rom 12:2).

The Importance of Knowing God's Word

The first step in preparing to win in our struggle against Satan and evil spirits is to know what God has said. If we don't know what God has said, we won't recognize Satan's lies. If we don't know what God has said, we won't be able to believe what He has said or do what He said.

The only way to get to know what God has said is to expend some effort. The more time you can spend reading and meditating upon the Bible, the better. You should attend a church regularly where God's Word is faithfully taught by a pastor who has a calling and an anointing to teach. Just because a church is "evangelical" doesn't necessarily mean anything. The question is, how often does the pastor read or quote from Scripture in his sermons? Does he preach on a *variety* of biblical themes? Does he preach only from Old Testament stories? Does he preach only from the gospels? Does he teach any other times besides Sunday mornings? A good pastor places a high priority on the preaching and teaching of the Word of God, because he knows God's Word is what equips, strengthens, and nourishes his people. Once you know what God has said and believe it, you are ready for battle.

Peter on Spiritual Warfare

The apostle Peter understood true, biblical spiritual warfare. Never in his epistles did he instruct Christians to pull down principalities and powers over cities. He did, however, instruct them to resist Satan's attacks against their personal lives, and he told them exactly how they should resist:

> Be of sober spirit, be on the alert. Your adversary, the devil, prowls about like a roaring lion, seeking someone to devour. But resist him, firm in your faith, knowing that the same experiences of suffering are being accomplished by your brethren who are in the world (1 Pet. 5:8-9).

Notice first that Peter indicated our position is one of defense, not offense. Satan is the one who is prowling around, not us. He is looking for us; we're not looking for him. Our job is not to attack but to resist.

Second, notice that Satan, like a lion, is seeking someone to *devour*. How could he possibly devour Christians? Did Peter mean that Satan could literally eat their flesh like a lion would? Obviously not. The only way Satan could devour a Christian is to deceive him into believing a lie that destroys his faith.

Third, notice Peter tells us to resist the devil through our faith. Our struggle is not a physical battle, and we can't fight Satan by swinging our fists in the air. He attacks us with lies, and we resist those lies by standing firm in our faith in God's Word. That, again, is scriptural spiritual warfare.

The Christians to whom Peter was writing were suffering some severe persecution, and thus were being tempted to renounce their faith in Christ. It is often when we are in the midst of adverse circumstances that Satan will attack with his doubts and lies. That is the time to stand firm in your faith. That is the "evil day" of which Paul wrote when you need to "put on the full armor of God, that you may be able to *stand firm* against the schemes of the devil (Eph. 6:11; italics mine).

James on Spiritual Warfare

The apostle James also mentioned something about spiritual warfare in his epistle. Did he tell the Christians that their prayers could determine the outcome of angelic battles? No. Did he tell them to pull down the spirits of lust, apathy, and drunkenness over their cities? No. Did he tell them to study the history of their cities so they could determine which kind of evil spirits have been there since the beginning? No.

James believed in scriptural, spiritual warfare, and so he wrote:

> Submit therefore to God. Resist the devil and he will flee from you (James 4:7; italics mine).

Once again, notice that the Christian's posture is one of defense—we are to resist, not attack. When we do, James promises us that Satan will flee. He has no reason to stick around a Christian who will not be persuaded to believe his lies, follow his suggestions, or yield to his temptations.

Notice also that James first instructed us to submit to God. We submit to God by submitting to His Word. Our resistance against Satan is based upon our submission to God's Word.

John on Spiritual Warfare

The apostle John also wrote about spiritual warfare in his first epistle. Did he tell us to be careful about having ceramic frogs by our fireplaces, lest we open our homes to an invasion of demons? No. Did he tell us to go up to the high places to tear down the devil's strongholds? No. Did he tell us how to cast the demon of anger out of Christians who sometimes get angry? No.

Rather, John, like Peter and James, only believed in biblical, spiritual warfare, and so his instructions are the same:

> Beloved, do not believe every spirit, but test the spirits to see whether they are from God; because many false prophets have gone out into the world. By

this you know the Spirit of God: every spirit that confesses that Jesus Christ has come in the flesh is from God; and every spirit that does not confess Jesus is not from God; and this is the spirit of the antichrist, of which you have heard that it is coming, and now it is already in the world. You are from God, little children, and have overcome them; because greater is He who is in you than he who is in the world. They are from the world; therefore they speak as from the world, and the world listens to them. We are from God; he who knows God listens to us; he who is not from God does not listen to us. By this we know the spirit of truth and the spirit of error (1 John 4:1-6).

Notice that John's entire discussion in these verses revolves around Satan's lies and God's truth. We are to test the spirits to see if they are from God, and the test is based on truth. Evil spirits will not admit that Jesus Christ came in the flesh. They are liars.

John also told us that we have overcome evil spirits. That is, as citizens of the kingdom of light, we are not under their dominion any longer. The greater one, Jesus, lives in us. People who have Christ living in them should not be afraid of demons.

John also said that the world listens to the evil spirits, which indicates that those evil spirits must be speaking. We know that they are not speaking audibly, but are planting lies in people's minds.

As followers of Christ, we should not be listening to the lies of evil spirits, and John states that those who know God are listening to us, because we have the truth; we have God's Word.

Again, notice that Satan's strategy is to persuade people to believe his lies. Satan cannot defeat us if we know and believe the truth. That is what scriptural, spiritual warfare is all about.

Paul on Spiritual Warfare

Paul, the apostle, also wrote about spiritual warfare. His most significant passage on the subject is found in the sixth chapter of Ephesians, and, since we have already examined it in detail in an earlier chapter, I won't exhaust you in this one.

This is Paul's famous passage about putting on the armor of God, a beautiful metaphor which describes how we can be protected from Satan's onslaughts by knowing and believing God's Word:

> Finally, be strong in the Lord, and in the strength of His might. Put on the full armor of God, *that you may be able to stand firm against the schemes of the devil.* For our struggle is not against flesh and blood, but against the rulers, against the powers, against the world forces of this darkness, against the spiritual forces of wickedness in the heavenly places. Therefore, take up the full armor of God, that you may be able to resist in the evil day, and having done everything, to stand firm. Stand firm therefore, having girded your loins with *truth*, and having put on the breastplate of righteousness, and having shod your feet with the preparation of the *gospel* of peace; in addition to all, taking up the *shield of faith* with which you will be able to extinguish all the flaming missiles of the evil one. And take the helmet of salvation, and the sword of the Spirit, which is *the word of God* (Eph. 6:10-17; italics mine)

Paul enumerates four categories of evil spirits, but categorizing them is obviously not his primary focus, nor should it be ours. Notice also that he makes no mention of demons of lust, demons of apathy, and so on, or even the prince of Rome.

Once again we see that our position is defensive; three times we are told to *stand firm*.

This is not a physical battle fought with physical weapons. Our armor is not built out of metal but out of truth.

Notice Paul's use of the words *truth, gospel, faith,* and *word of God.*

Since we protect ourselves with truth, the flaming missiles which evil spirits are firing at us can only be lies. With the shield of faith we can extinguish every single one.

Jesus on Spiritual Warfare

Finally we come to what Jesus taught about spiritual warfare.

First of all, He demonstrated what biblical spiritual warfare is all about when he encountered Satan in His wilderness temptation, an incident we have already considered earlier in this chapter. Jesus' warfare with the devil revolved around what God had said. Satan's attack came through suggestions, doubts, and temptations. Jesus overcame him in every instance by knowing, quoting, and obeying God's Word.

In the parable of the sower and the soils, Jesus revealed to us that it is Satan who steals the Word of God when it is sown into certain people's hearts. Of course, the only way Satan could steal God's Word once it is sown in someone's heart is by persuading that person to believe one of his lies.

Jesus also revealed to us that Satan is a liar by nature and even called him "the father of lies" (John 8:44). Likewise, He told His disciples to be careful what they listened to (Mark 4:24), and promised them that if they would abide in His word, they would know the truth, and the truth would make them free (John 8:31-32).

Jesus proclaimed, "I am the light of the world; he who follows Me shall not walk in the darkness" (John 8:12). Light is symbolic for truth, darkness for deception. It is only as we follow Jesus, knowing and acting on what He has said, that we escape from the darkness of Satan's deception. That is biblical, spiritual warfare.

Finally, on the cross Jesus rendered Satan powerless in regard to spiritual death, and now anyone on Earth can potentially escape from Satan's grasp. Each person, however, must know and believe the gospel if he is to escape, which makes the very act of salvation an act of spiritual warfare. Every time someone hears the gospel there is a spiritual struggle, and every time someone believes the gospel, a spiritual victory is won. To maintain that victory, the Christian must continue to believe the truth, even when Satan and his minions attack with their "flaming missiles" (Eph. 6:16).

Satan is Persistent

As long as Satan and his evil spirits are around, we will have to struggle against them. And just because we have won a victory today is no guarantee that Satan will not be back to try again tomorrow. Jesus informed us of the devil's persistence:

> "Now when the unclean spirit goes out of a man, it passes through waterless places, seeking rest, and does not find it. Then it says, 'I will return to my house from which I came'; and when it comes, it finds it unoccupied, swept, and put in order. Then it goes, and takes along with it seven other spirits more wicked than itself, and they go in and live there; and the last state of that man becomes worse than the first. That is the way it will also be with this evil generation" (Matt. 12:43-45).

This evil spirit who was cast out eventually came back, and unfortunately, he discovered his former "house" was "unoccupied, swept, and put in order." In order to keep the demon out, the man needed to be indwelt by the Holy Spirit and filled with God's Word so he could stand firm in faith against the evil spirit.

We would do a person a disservice if we cast a demon out of him and then did not lead him to Christ and teach him how to resist the devil by faith in God's Word. Once he is born again, his body becomes the temple of the Holy Spirit, and once he knows what God has said, he is equipped for spiritual battle. By the same token, every Christian needs to be prepared for a demonic attack, so he can resist "in the evil day" (Eph. 6:13).

Faith is the Key

Knowing God's Word is not enough to win in spiritual battle. The key is *truly believing* what God has said. This is true in resisting the devil and in casting out of demons. For example, consider again an example we have examined previously, when Jesus gave His twelve disciples "authority over unclean spirits, to cast them out" (Matt. 10:1). Yet we find them, seven chapters later, unable to cast a demon out of an epileptic boy.[1] When Jesus learned of their failure, He lamented:

> "*O unbelieving* and perverted generation, how long shall I be with you? How long shall I put up with you?" (Matt. 17:17; italics mine).

It was their unbelief that Jesus bemoaned. Moreover, when His disciples later questioned Him as to why they were unable to cast the demon out, Jesus responded, "Because of the littleness of your faith" (Matt. 17:20). Thus we see that their authority to cast out demons did not work apart from their faith.

Our success in casting out demons and resisting the devil is dependent upon our faith in God's Word. If we truly do believe what God has said, then we will talk like it and act like it. Dogs chase people who run from them, and it is the same with the devil. If you'll run, the devil will chase you. If you'll stand firm in your faith, the devil will flee from you (Jas. 4:7).

No doubt the apostles' lack of faith would have been very evident to any observer, as they tried but failed to deliver that boy from a demon. If that demon put on the same show for the disciples as he performed in front of Jesus, throwing the boy into a "violent convulsion" (Luke 9:42) and causing him to foam at the mouth (Mark 9:20), it is possible that the disciples' faith turned to fear. They were perhaps paralyzed by what they witnessed.

---

[1] We should be very cautious in assuming that all epilepsy is caused by an indwelling evil spirit.

Faith, however, is not moved by what is seen, but rather, is moved only by what God has said. "We walk by faith, *not by sight*" (2 Cor. 5:7; italics mine). God cannot lie (Tit. 1:2), and so even if our circumstances seemingly contradict what God has said, we should remain steadfast in faith.

Notice that Jesus delivered the boy in just a few seconds. He did it by faith. He did not waste His time conducting a "deliverance session." Those who have faith in their God-given authority don't need to spend hours casting out a demon.

Moreover, there is no record that Jesus screamed at the demon. Those who have faith don't need to scream. Neither did Jesus repeatedly command the demon to come out. One command was sufficient. A second command would have been an admission of doubt.

Who You Believe—the Secret of Spiritual Success

The battleground of our spiritual battle is not in the heavenly places, but in our own minds. Either we are thinking about and believing Satan's thoughts, or thinking about and believing what God has said. Our thoughts about ourselves, about others, about God, about our circumstances, and so on, are divine or demonic. Our faith is ultimately either in what God has said, or what Satan has said.

Jesus exhorted us, "Have faith in God" (Mark 11:22). That is not only the secret to successful prayer, but the secret for successful spiritual warfare. Believe what God says. If you do, Satan and his evil spirits will have no chance of overcoming you.

Epilogue

I'm overjoyed that God is in control, and that the outcome of some supposed cosmic battle between God and Satan doesn't depend upon us.

I'm glad that God is all-powerful and all-wise, and that His eternal plan is perfect.

I'm thrilled to know that Satan doesn't have any authority that is beyond God's authority, and that God is truly sovereign, the "Lord of heaven and earth" (Matt. 11:25).

I'm happy that demons can't possess us when we sin, and that we can overcome the devil simply by trusting and obeying God.

I'm thankful that we don't need to fast to gain victory over Satan, or fear that we are destined to suffer because of some supposed curse placed upon our great-grandparents.

And I'm elated that by knowing the truth, we have been set free from having to believe *any* of Satan's many lies (John 8:32).

Whether you have realized it or not, while you were reading this book you were involved in spiritual warfare. Just as the devil said to Eve, "Has God said....?", no doubt Satan placed doubt-filled questions in your mind as you read. The fact that you've made it this far, however, is a good indication that you are a sure winner in your spiritual battle. You believe the truth, and Satan has no avenue to overcome you. Congratulations! Keep your armor on, and rejoice that someday soon our struggle will be over for- ever!

...then comes the end, when He [Jesus] delivers up the kingdom to the God and Father, *when He has abolished all rule and all authority and power.* For He must reign until He has put all His enemies under His feet (1 Cor. 15:24-25; italics mine).

And the devil who deceived them was thrown into the lake of fire and brimstone...and they will be tormented day and night forever and ever (Rev. 20:10).

Also by David Kirkwood...

Your Best Year Yet is a daily devotional-commentary that will help you read through the entire Bible in one year. This easy-to-read devotional follows the reading plan of the *One Year Bible®*, and contains inspirational reflections, historical background notes, and life-changing applications for each day's reading from the Old and New Testaments. Discover fresh insights from God's Word to help make this ...*Your Best Year Yet*! (ISBN 088-419-2741, 480 pages, Trade paper, $15.95)

Lead your loved ones to Christ by giving them *Forgive Me For Waiting so Long to Tell You This*. In this easy-to-understand book, David Kirkwood shares the gospel in a logical, biblical, and *very* convincing manner. Your friends and loved ones will be respectfully confronted with the amazing love of God and the claims of Christ. They'll understand the significance of Jesus' death. And they may very well receive Jesus as their Savior and Lord. (ISBN 096-296-2503, 132 pages, Trade paper, $6.95)

Christ's Incredible Cross is an unveiling of the Bible's central theme—Jesus' sacrificial death. In a warm and readable style, David Kirkwood presents a concise, chronological study of the most important—yet often most neglected—truth in Scripture. Your appreciation of Jesus' sacrificial death will grow to new heights as you discover amazing biblical revelation about *Christ's Incredible Cross*! (ISBN 096-296-2511, 168 pages, Trade paper, $7.95)

The Christian Disciple's Manual is packed with biblical information that is vital for every believer to understand. Whether you are a brand new Christian or have been walking with the Lord for years, you'll gain scriptural insight that will enrich your life and draw you closer to God. This concise manual for Christian growth contains thirty-one chapters, including *The New Birth, Discipleship, In Christ Realities, Fundamentals of Faith, The Healing Ministry of Jesus, The Fruit of the Spirit, The Gifts of the Spirit, How to Defeat the Devil, How to be Led by the Holy Spirit, Prosperity and Stewardship, The Christian Family, The Afterlife, the End Times, Intercessory Prayer,* and many more. (ISBN 096-296-252X, 294 pages, Trade Paper, $8.95)

"If God loves me, why am I facing these difficulties?" "What did I do to deserve this?" "Am I being chastened by God or attacked by the devil?" "Is God trying to teach me something in all this?" If you've ever found yourself asking those kinds of questions, then *God's Tests* is the perfect book for you. David Kirkwood offers satisfying, understandable answers to life's trials and dilemmas. Drawing from the many biblical examples of God testing individuals, he concludes that victory is always God's ultimate will, and that there is no reason for any believer to remain in a valley of defeat. Your faith in God can deliver you, and you can pass every test! (ISBN 096-296-2538, 224 pages, Trade Paper, $7.95)

All of these titles are available through your local Christian bookstore. You can also obtain them directly from ETHNOS Press, P.O. Box 0446, Library, PA 15129, USA. Please enclose 12% postage and handling with your order.

For a free catalog of teaching tapes
by David Kirkwood, write to:

ETHNOS Press
P.O. Box 0446
Library, PA 15129   U.S.A.